# THE SHEP
## Hedd Wyn (F

**Edited and Introduction by**
**Gruffudd Antur**

**Poetry Translator and Adaptor:**
**Howard Huws**

**Photographs for Poetry Section:**
**Keith O'Brien**

First published in 2017

© publication: Gwasg Carreg Gwalch 2017

All rights reserved. No part of this publication may be reproduced, stored in a retrieval system, or transmitted in any form or by any means, electronic, electrostatic, magnetic tape, mechanical, photocopying, recording, or otherwise, without prior permission of the authors of the works herein.

ISBN: 978-1-84527-594-5

Cover design: Eleri Owen
Cover image: Keith O'Brien

Published by Gwasg Carreg Gwalch,
12 Iard yr Orsaf, Llanrwst, Wales LL26 0EH
tel: 01492 642031
email: llanrwst@carreg-gwalch.com
website: www.carreg-gwalch.com

Published with the financial support of the Welsh Books Council

## Acknowledgements
*Photographs*
*Keith O'Brien, Trawsfynydd: pages 1, 2, 20, 24-88*
*Ymddiriedolaeth yr Ysgwrn, Awdurdod Parc Cenedlaethol Eryri (Snowdonia National Park Authority): pages 6, 8, 14*
*Comisiwn Brenhinol Henebion Cymru*
*(Royal Commission on the Ancient and Historical Monuments of Wales): page 91*

# Contents

**Introduction** *Gruffudd Antur*   4

**Hedd Wyn – a timeline** *Naomi Jones*   10

**The Shepherd's Poems**   25
- War   27
- In an album   28
- Mute harp   33
- The black spot   34
- An end to roaming   37
- Gwenfron and I   39
- Facing the tempest   43
- A mother's burial   45
- Patriotism (Extracts)   46
- To die young   53
- A wish   54
- The dawn   56
- The sun on the mountain   59
- Y Moelwyn   60
- The paths of war   63
- Litherland Camp   64
- A marriage in wartime   65
- To the scattered children of Trawsfynydd, 1914   69
- The children of Trawsfynydd, 1915   71
- Memorial Flowers
  - The death of a little girl   72
  - Griff Llewelyn   75
  - Unforgotten   76
  - The great sacrifice   79
- To die far from home   83
- The inviting   85
- The hero (Extract)   87
- A memory   89

**Yr Ysgwrn 2017** *Naomi Jones*   90

**Hedd Wyn** (Extract)   96
*R. Williams Parry*

# Introduction

Due to his untimely, tragic death, Hedd Wyn gained immortality. A century after his death as a young man on a blood-soaked battlefield far away from home, one of many thousands of lives wasted that very same day, his name remains seared on an entire nation's memory, his home has become a place of pilgrimage, and his story continues to anger and inspire us. It may be said that Hedd Wyn – or the Hedd Wyn that we have come to know, at least – was born on the battlefield; his death has become an integral part of his story and his legacy. This very death has come to embody the impact of the First World War on Wales; all of rural Wales' losses have been condensed into one loss where we have, on the one hand, a promising young poet from the heartland of Meirionnydd, a poet who was quickly gaining a reputation for himself and, on the other hand, the iron fist of the Great War. And by dying only a few weeks before the National Eisteddfod in Birkenhead in 1917, the Eisteddfod which his ode had been deemed worthy of its Chair, his story gained its perfect, cruel twist in its tail.

But in the midst of this tragic, enchanting story about the poet, it is all too easy, sometimes, to forget about the poetry itself, and to think that Hedd Wyn was a prodigy who was lost far too early, lost before he could fulfil his potential. This does him a great disservice. With the dawn of the twentieth century a new, exciting generation of poets emerged, poets such as T. Gwynn Jones, R. Williams Parry and T. H. Parry-Williams, who were deeply rooted in their ancient tradition but who had the ability to grab this tradition by the scruff of its neck and put it back on its feet. Welsh poetry had for many decades revolved in a directionless quagmire of lengthy, dry, pseudo-philosophical odes; this generation, however, of which Hedd Wyn was becoming an ever-growing part, changed things for the better. And even though he did not live to see the day, Hedd Wyn fulfilled his lifelong dream of winning the Chair at the National Eisteddfod, the powerful significance of which served as a reminder of a time gone by when the chief poet would be given a seat at the king's table, a time when Welsh poetry was a medium fit for kings. And he had been eyeing it for some time: as a fledgling poet

*The Eisteddfod at Birkenhead, September 1917*

he had practiced his craft under the guiding hand of his teacher, William Morris, and he quickly became proficient in the art of *cynghanedd*, the ancient Welsh craft which employs repetition of consonants and rhymes within the confines of intricate metres. On his way to fulfilling his ambition he won a roomful of Chairs from local eisteddfodau, and came within a whisker of winning the national Chair in 1916 for his ode to the abbey of Strata Florida. In 1917, however, when a dark, mystical ode to '*Yr Arwr*' ('The Hero'), submitted by '*Fleur-de-lis*' (in other words, Hedd Wyn), was deemed worthy of the Chair at the National Eisteddfod in Birkenhead, it meant that its author had fulfilled his life's ambition.

'*Yr Arwr*' is, therefore, an ode of great importance; its title and its significance are part and parcel of Hedd Wyn's story, but even so, only a few lines, if any at all, have stuck in the nation's memory. Even though it was to be the symbolic peak of his career, it can scarcely be regarded as his best work. On the other hand, of course, some of his poems are, without a shadow of doubt, among the most famous and most significant Welsh poems of the twentieth century. They can, perhaps, be divided into two sections. Firstly, we have lyrical poems celebrating the people and to the landscape of Trawsfynydd, poems that show not only unabated love for his land and his people but also his ability to avoid sinking into blind romanticism where others would have slipped. His main themes were land, nature and people, and the close interconnection between the three; the poet's world was here unspoilt and not marred in any way by the troubles of the world, but this was merely the calm before the storm. After the War broke out, his voice became tinged by a cynical, dark, bitter note, but his themes – land, nature and people – and values remained constant. Something extraordinary occurs in these poems. Anybody who is familiar with the poet's story cannot fail to sense that these poems are imbued with an immense force: this is due to the conflation of the poetry and the poet's own story, and the hard irony screams like a war-horn in every word. It

*Stone wall craftsmen at Yr Ysgwrn, 2016*

*The Shepherd War Poet*

is impossible not to read these poems in the light of the events of July 1917, and as we read we realise that the poetry has turned into an elegy for the poet himself. The most obvious example, perhaps, is the following *englyn*, '*Nid â'n Ango*' ('Unforgotten'):

> His sacrifice abided – his dear face
> > Ever recollected,
> > Though Germany has tainted
> Her iron fist a bloody red.

Its intended subject was Hedd Wyn's friend, D. O. Evans, but the poet himself quickly became the subject of his own words. Similarly, in '*Rhyfel*' ('War'), every 'poor man's croft' that was torn apart by the Great War came to be represented by Hedd Wyn's own home, Yr Ysgwrn. And this cruel irony permeates even further. Even the tamest, least melancholic poems concerning nothing more than the simple beauty of his beloved Trawsfynydd are tainted with the darkness of the poet's death and the filth of the trenches in which he died.

Of course, Hedd Wyn was not a lone voice in the darkness. Other talented and revered Welsh poets wrote about the war, including some who had first-hand experience of its terrors, but this unusual and potent marriage between the poet and his poetry means that Hedd Wyn's war poetry hits harder than any written by his contemporaries. We see a similar story in the case of another poet who died on the same day as Hedd Wyn, Francis Ledwidge. The stories of both poets are strikingly similar: they were both peasant poets who were born in similar circumstances in the same year and died on the same day in the very same battle; Ledwidge, nicknamed 'the poet of the blackbirds', is commemorated by a plaque in his home village, Slane, in County Meath, which bears the following words:

> He shall not hear the bittern cry
> > In the wild sky, where he is lain,
> > Nor voices of the sweeter birds
> Above the wailing of the rain.

These are Ledwidge's own words, taken from his elegy to Thomas MacDonagh, one of the leaders of the 1916 Easter Rising, but as in the case of Hedd Wyn, whose words in '*Rhyfel*' ('War') are eerily reminiscent of

*Demolishing the old agricultural shed and building the new one at Yr Ysgwrn, 2016*

Ledwidge's, the words have long been appropriated in memory of the poet himself and his lost generation. A little over a year after Hedd Wyn and Ledwige's deaths, another poet, Wilfred Owen, died; Owen's poetry, like Hedd Wyn's and Ledwige's, shattered the British ideal of the honour of war. These three poets were thrown from different directions into the same slaughterhouse, but their reactions to what they saw was essentially the same, and strangely, despite their tragic stories, it is to the words of poets such as these three, mowed down by the machine they so detested, that we turn in order to look for a glimmer of light amid such sheer darkness.

When looking back at something as incomprehensible as the First World War, concentrating on the scale of one particular loss makes it easier for us to understand the grief as a whole. We remember this particular poet from Meirionnydd because he embodies the losses experienced by Wales, the Welsh language and its culture as a whole, and we celebrate the safeguarding and the restoration of his home, Yr Ysgwrn, because it forms a peaceful, living memorial to the poet – and indeed to all the men of Trawsfynydd and beyond who lost their lives – in his own square mile. We also cherish his poems because the values they exhibit – the love of country, people, friendship and peace – are ones that we uphold earnestly when we remember and try to understand what happened a century ago. It is these values that will ensure that Hedd Wyn's sacrifice, and that of his contemporaries, will never be forgotten.

Gruffudd Antur

*Gruffudd Antur is a contemporary young Welsh poet from Meirionnydd, born and bred in Llanuwchllyn near Bala, eastwards over the hills from Trawsfynydd. He is already well-versed in the poetic tradition, climbing the same ladder of learning and practicing his craft as Hedd Wyn did a century earlier.*

# Hedd Wyn – a timeline

### 1887
Ellis Humphrey Evans, a poet shepherd from Trawsfynydd, was born the first of fourteen children, on the January 13th, 1887, in his grandmother's small cottage at Penlan, Trawsfynydd. He was the son of Evan and Mary Evans (nee Morris) and known to Trawsfynydd folk as 'Elsyn Yr Ysgwrn', although he is better known to most as 'Hedd Wyn' (Blessed Place).

At four months of age, Ellis and his parents moved to Yr Ysgwrn, a farm on the southern slopes of Cwm Prysor, which had been home to his father's family since 1830.

### 1888-1907
Evan and Mary's other thirteen children were born at Yr Ysgwrn between 1888 and 1907: David (Dafydd), Mary, Kate (Cati), Llewelyn Lewis (the first), Sarah Ann, Maggie (Magi), Llewelyn Lewis (the second), Robert Llewelyn (Robin or Bob), Evan Morris, Ann and Enid, as well as two stillborn children. The children's names were recorded in the family Bible, still kept on the dresser in the kitchen at Yr Ysgwrn. Three children were lost as infants: Llewelyn Lewis (the first), Sarah Ann and Llewelyn Lewis (the second).

### 1899
Hedd Wyn received a fragmented formal education at Trawsfynydd School. He was registered there in 1892 and the log book's last record of him was made in 1899, when he was twelve. During bad weather, or if any important tasks needed to be done at home, he would stay at home on the farm for the day. Education and culture were, however, revered in the home and in the community, and through Chapel society, Sunday School and reading widely, Ellis had a rich cultural background.

### 1900
There was plenty of work at home at Yr Ysgwrn for Ellis, and he didn't have to search for employment elsewhere. Ellis was given free rein by his parents to devote his time to composing poetry, and enjoyed musing in peace at Yr Ysgwrn. He

*1. The kitchen range at Yr Ysgwrn, 2005;*
*2. Yr Ysgwrn, 1990;*
*3. The farm name in poetic alphabet*

*The Shepherd War Poet*

12  *The Shepherd War Poet*

was devoted to Trawsfynydd and many of his poems were inspired by his surroundings. When Dafydd, Hedd Wyn's brother, left school, he also came home to work, followed by Mary, Cati and Magi who did domestic work at home, while the younger children, Bob, Evan, Ann and Enid were still at school.

Hedd Wyn won his first poetry competition for composing an *englyn* (a 4-line traditional Welsh verse in strict metre) to the peat stack ('Y Das Fawn') at the age of 12, at the Ebenezer Chapel literary meeting.

### 1907
He won his first Chair at the Bala Eisteddfod yn 1907, with his poem, 'Y *Dyffryn*' ('The Valley').

### 1909
At the age of twenty-two, Hedd Wyn gained employment at the Abercynon coal mine, residing at 46 Abercynon Terrace. The hours were long, the work was hard and the *hiraeth* (homesickness)

1. *The family (Hedd Wyn: back, left);*
2. *Ellis and Gerald, the great-nephews;*
3. *Bob, Ellis' younger brother; 4. Ellis*

 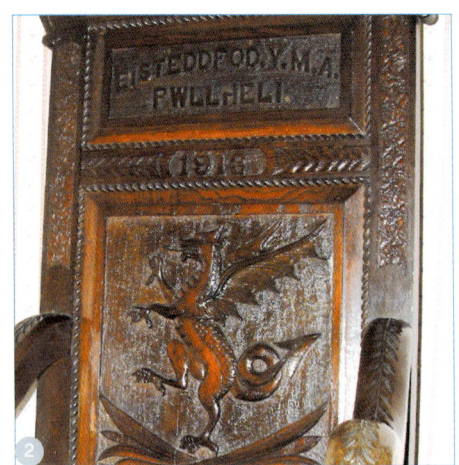

unbearable. Hedd Wyn only remained there for three months.

## 1910
On New Year's Day 1910, Dafydd, Hedd Wyn's brother, sailed from Liverpool to Sydney, Australia. He worked there as a farmhand for a while, before moving on to New Zealand. He lived and worked here for several years, dying in 1918 at the age of thirty, of the Spanish flu.

## 1910
A special inauguration was held at the Blaenau Ffestinog Hall to present several local poets to Bryfdir (Humphrey Jones), Bard of the Gorsedd. The ceremony was followed by an investiture on the shores of Llyn Morynion, Llan Ffestiniog and there Bryfdir gave Ellis Humphrey Evans the name by which he is better known today: Hedd Wyn. Thereafter, he continued to compose and publish his poems in the local press, including *Y Glorian* and *Y Rhedegydd*.

*1. and 2. Early Chairs won by Hedd Wyn;*
*3. 'Y Gadair Ddu', 1917;*
*4. Memorial on the site of the 1917 Eisteddfod*

*Hedd Wyn*

# ARWYR TRAWSFYNYDD

| | | | | |
|---|---|---|---|---|
| G. Llew Morris. | J. Morris. (L.F.) | W. Evans (Canadians) | Tom Morris. (R.W.F.) | R. Morris. (Welsh Regt) |
| E.R. Parry (S.W.B.) | Watkin Jones (Welsh Regt) | Major Evans (R.W.F.) | W. Llew Jones (R.W.F.) | W.J. Davies (M.G.C.) |
| O. Evans (R.W.F.) | Rd. Williams (R.W.F.) | Ellis Evans (Hedd Wyn)(R.W.F.) | R.E. Phillips (R.W.F.) | Evan Williams (R.W.F.) |
| J. Williams (R.W.F.) | Moses Lewis (A.S.C.) | Lieut. Azariah Phillips (R.F.C.) | Ellis J. Jones. (R.E.) | Tom Evans (R.W.F.) |

MEWN ANGOF NI HAINT FOD
*Ceiriog*

### 1913-16

Hedd Wyn continued to compete in eisteddfodau and poetry competitions and made quite a success of it, adding another four Chairs to his collection: Pwllheli (1913), Llanuwchllyn (1913), Pontardawe (1915) and Llanuwchllyn (1915). Hedd Wyn's ambitions were set on the National Eisteddfod Chair and he competed for it for the first time in 1914, the year in which the First World War broke out and the Eisteddfod was postponed for a year until 1915. '*Eryri*' was the theme of the competition and Hedd Wyn entered an ode to the mythology of the surroundings that were so close to his heart. Although he received a harsh adjudication in that competition, he perservered and had better success at the Aberystwyth Natonal Eisteddfod in 1916, coming second with his ode, '*Ystrad Fflur*' ('Strata Florida').

### 1916-1917

In January 1916, the British Government passed the first Military Service Act, which brought in conscription. It decreed that every unmarried man between the ages of eighteen and forty must join the armed forces. Despite Hedd Wyn's arguments that he contributed to the war effort through his agricultural work at home at Yr Ysgwrn, because his younger brother Bob was about to turn eighteen, the authorities insisted that one of Yr Ysgwrn's boys must join the army. Before being forced to join, Hedd Wyn went to Blaenau Ffestiniog to enlist in January 1917.

### Spring 1917

Despite composing a poem called '*Gwersyll Litherland*' ('Litherland Camp') during his training, Hedd Wyn found little inspiration in the barracks. He appears to have written about half of his ode, '*Yr Arwr*' ("The Hero") before arriving at the camp and had a further opportunity to complete it while home at Yr Ysgwrn, on leave from the army, to help with the ploughing.

### June 1917

Hedd Wyn's battallion, the 15th Royal Welch Fusiliers sailed to France on June 9th, 1917. Arriving at the port of Le Havre in France, the battalion moved on to the military camp on the outskirts of Rouen and then to Fléchin, a village on the

*Some of the Trawsfynydd men lost in the First World War*

Franco-Belgian border, at the beginning of July.

## July 1917

In the roasting heat that characterised the summer of 1917, Hedd Wyn and his battalion left Fléchin on July 15th, travelling for two days, to reach two camps on the banks of the Yser Canal in Flanders. There, the battalion practised and prepared for the Battle of Pilkem Ridge. This would be one of the bloodiest battles of the First World War. At 3.50am on the morning of July 31st, 1917, the soldiers went over the top, into a boggy no man's land, in atrocious rain and dark fog. There are various accounts of how Hedd Wyn was killed, but he was apparently injured by an exploding shell and died while being transported to hospital.

## August 1917

Hedd Wyn was buried in the Artillery Wood Cemetery in plot 2, row F, grave 11, a stone's throw from the grave of Irish poet Francis Ledwidge. Hedd Wyn and Francis were of the same age, of similar poetic temperament, and were killed on the same day in the same battle within a quarter of a mile of each other. Around three weeks later, the official news arrived at Yr Ysgwrn, informing the family of the death of their son, Private Ellis Humphrey Evans.

## September 1917

A short fortnight later, on September 6th, the National Eisteddfod was held at Birkenhead Park. During the chairing ceremony and in the presence of a bustling, thousand-strong audience *Fleur-de-lis* was called to stand on his feet. Once. Twice. Three times. No one stood. Then, Archdruid Dyfed announced that *Fleur-de-lis* was the nom de plume of Hedd Wyn, and that he had been killed six weeks previously, somewhere in France. The Chair, expertly carved by Belgian refugee Eugeen Vanfleteren was draped in a black cloth and has been known ever since as *Y Gadair Ddu* (the Black Chair). The grief of a nation overcame Birkenhead Park that afternoon: the shadow of the Great War fell over the Eisteddfod and, immediately, Hedd Wyn became a symbol of Wales' tragic losses during the War and his empty

*1. Hedd Wyn's grave, Artillery Wood Cemetery;*
*2. Hedd Wyn's statue at Trawsfynydd*

The Shepherd War Poet

Chair symbolic of empty chairs in homes throughout Wales.

### 1918

Soon after his death, Hedd Wyn's friends and prominent poets gathered to compile his poems, and in 1918, his *Cerddi'r Bugail* anthology was published, with profits donated to the Hedd Wyn memorial fund. The anthology proved to be so popular that a second edition was published in 1921.

20    *The Shepherd War Poet*

## Later

With the proceeds of the memorial fund, Londoner L. S. Merrifield was commissioned to produce a memorial statue depicting Hedd Wyn, looking towards Yr Ysgwrn. Hedd Wyn's biography was published by his friend William Morris in 1969. This was followed by further biographies of Hedd Wyn by Alan Llwyd in 1992, 2009 and 2015. Paul Turner and Alan Llwyd's biopic, *Hedd Wyn* was released in 1992 and was nominated for an Academy Award (Oscar) in the Foreign Language Film category.

In 1992, a Hedd Wyn memorial plaque was unveiled in Boesinghe, Belgium by his niece and nephew, Mrs Malo Bampton and Mr Meurig Jones Morris. Since Hedd Wyn's death, his family have kept the door of Yr Ysgwrn open to visitors who are fascinated by his story, most recently by his nephews, Gerald and the late Ellis Williams. 2004 saw the official opening, by Gerald Williams, of Llys Ednowain Heritage Centre in Trawsfynydd where Hedd Wyn's wooden burial cross is now displayed. In 2012, Yr Ysgwrn was purchased by the Snowdonia National Park Authority for the nation, with the aim of keeping the door open and the legacy alive.

## 2017

The re-opening of Yr Ysgwrn as a museum, with a series of events and activities to mark the centenary of Hedd Wyn's death and the Eisteddfod of the Black Chair.

*1. Ellis' wooden cross, now at Llys Ednowain;*
*2. Gerald at Yr Ysgwrn*

22   The Shepherd War Poet

1. Ellis' memorial plaques at Hagebos, Flanders;
2. Part of the memorial exhibition at the restaurant at Hagebos;
3. The Welsh National Memorial in Flanders with its garden of daffodils

# The Shepherd's Poems

## A selection of Hedd Wyn's verse in Welsh and in translation

*The old railway at Cwm Prysor*

## Rhyfel

Gwae fi fy myw mewn oes mor ddreng,
 A Duw ar drai ar orwel pell;
O'i ôl mae dyn, yn deyrn a gwreng,
 Yn codi ei awdurdod hell.

Pan deimlodd fyned ymaith Dduw
 Cyfododd gledd i ladd ei frawd;
Mae sŵn yr ymladd ar ein clyw,
 A'i gysgod ar fythynnod tlawd.

Mae'r hen delynau genid gynt
 Ynghrog ar gangau'r helyg draw,
A gwaedd y bechgyn lond y gwynt,
 A'u gwaed yn gymysg efo'r glaw.

## War

Woe that I live at this fell time,
 When God has ebbed so far away;
And man into His place did climb,
 Both king and churl, to demand sway.

When he felt God no longer near,
 He raised the killing sword aloft:
The sound of battle fills the ear,
 Its shadow's on the poor man's croft.

The ancient harps which once were played
 Now hang on willows over there,
And in the rain boys' blood is made
 To flow; their screaming fills the air.

*Winter, Trawsfynydd*

*Hedd Wyn*

**Mewn album**

Cerdda rhai adwaenom heno
    Ewrop bell ddi-gainc,
Lle mae dafnau gwaed ar fentyll
    Prydain Fawr a Ffrainc.

Cysga eraill a adwaenom
    Yn y fynwent brudd;
Lle mae'r awel fyth yn wylo,
    Wylo nos a dydd.

Troeog iawn yw llwybrau bywyd
    Megis gwynt yr hwyr;
Pa le'n cludir ninnau ganddo,
    Duw yn unig ŵyr.

# In an album

Tonight our friends walk through a distant
    Europe where song lies dead.
Where British uniforms and French
    Are spattered red.

Others whom we know are sleeping
    Rank on rank in clay
Where the wind forever weeps,
    Weeps night and day.

Like an evening breeze, life's path
    Ever twisting, turning goes;
As to where the road may take us,
    God only knows.

*Llyn Trawsfynydd*

## Telyn fud

Gwelais un ymhlith y defaid
    Derfyn hafaidd ddydd;
Gwelais degwch rhos bendigaid
    Ar ei ieuanc rudd;
Canai'r chwa wrth fynd a dyfod
    Rhwng y grug a'r dail;
Canai yntau'n ddiarwybod
    Gyda'i lais di-ail.

Gwelais ef yng ngŵyl ei henfro
    Gynt yn canu cân,
Gwelais wedyn ei arwisgo
    Â llawryfau glân;
Clywais sŵn ei lais yn torri,
    Fin allorau'r Iôr,
Megis sŵn ewynnau lili
    O tan wynt y môr.

Wedyn gwelais ef yn edwi
    Tan y barrug gwyn,
Ambell islais pêr yn torri
    Tros ei wefus syn;
Yna gwelais ddyfod trosto
    Olau'r machlud drud;
Hithau'r gân am byth yn peidio
    Ar ei wefus fud.

Sefais wrth ei fedd un hwyrddydd,
    Bedd y gobaith glân
Wybu londer plant y mynydd,
    Wybu ganu cân;
A phe medrwn torrwn innau
    Ar ei feddfaen fud
Ddarlun telyn gyda'i thannau
    Wedi torri i gyd.

*Dramatic rays above Trawsfynydd ('God's fingers')*

## Mute harp

In summertime, I saw among
The sheep, as day drew to a close,
One who bore on cheeks so young
The blessed beauty of the rose;
As the breeze sang in its wafting
Through the heather and the grass,
So, unaware, he wandered, singing
In a voice none could surpass.

I saw him as he competed,
Singing in his village hall,
And I saw his brows garlanded
With the victor's laurels all.
I heard at God's altars breaking
Like a wave, his voice, as he
Sang as foam comes lightly drifting
Pure and white from off the sea.

Afterwards, I saw him fading
In the white frost's grip,
A sweet undertone came breaking
From his startled lip.
I saw on his face the colour
Of the sunset's blush,
And the song was stilled forever:
Mute, eternal hush.

I stood by his grave one evening,
The grave of hope so pure,
That knew the joy that comes of singing
Joys of life upon the moor;
And if I could, I'd carve surely
On his mute memorial stone,
An image of a harp so lovely
But with broken strings alone.

*Yr Wyddfa (Snowdon) from Feidiogydd, Trawsfynydd*

*Hedd Wyn*

## Y blotyn du

Nid oes gennym hawl ar y sêr,
    Na'r lleuad hiraethus chwaith,
Na'r cwmwl o aur a ymylch
    Yng nghanol y glesni maith.

Nid oes gennym hawl ar ddim byd
    Ond ar yr hen ddaear wyw;
A honno sy'n anhrefn i gyd
    Yng nghanol gogoniant Duw.

## The black spot

We haven't a claim on the stars,
    Nor on the lonesome moon,
Nor on the golden cloud that bathes
    Amidst the unbounded blue.

We haven't a claim in the world,
    There's nothing that's yours or mine,
But the dear old earth, all gone to rack
    Amidst the glory Divine.

*Capel Penstryd*

### Gorffen crwydro

Ceraist ti grwydro gwledydd pellennig,
    Y gwledydd sy 'mhell tros y don;
Weithiau dychwelit i'th gartre mynyddig
    A'th galon yn ysgafn a llon.

Gwelsom di ennyd cyn dychwel ohonot
    I'r rhyfel sy'n crynu y byd;
Nodau y gwlatgar a'r beiddgar oedd ynot,
    Y nodau sy'n costio mor ddrud.

Fe chwyth y corwynt tros fryniau Trawsfynydd
    O'th ôl fel yn athrist ei gainc;
Tithau yng nghwmni'r fataliwn ddihysbydd
    Sy'n cysgu'n ddifreuddwyd yn Ffrainc.

## An end to roaming

You loved to roam the distant lands,
    The countries beyond the sea,
Sometimes you'd return to your highland home,
    And so light of heart you'd be.

We saw you awhile before you returned
    To the war that makes the world quake,
Bearing the marks so dearly bought
    For your country and bravery's sake.

The storm rages over Trawsfynydd's hills
    After you, as if it would weep;
You, who with numberless battalions in France
    Lie there in a dreamless sleep.

*Cwm Prysor*

*Hedd Wyn*

## Gwenfron a mi

Cydgerdded wnâi Gwenfron a minnau un tro,
A chwerthin yr awel ym mrigau y fro;
'Roedd lloer yn yr awyr, a lloer yn y llyn,
Ac eos yn canu o laslwyn y glyn;
A serch ar ei orau ar noson fel hyn.
Ac yno yn suon yr awel a'r lli
Gwnaed cymod annatod rhwng Gwenfron a mi.

Flynyddoedd maith wedyn 'roedd coedydd y glyn
Heb ddeilen, nac awel, dan eira gwyn, gwyn;
'Roedd oriau ieuenctid ers talwm ar ffo,
A mil o ofalon yn llanw y fro,
A'r corwynt yn ubain o'r coed yn ei dro;
Ond chwerwed gaeafau, a rhued y lli,
Ni thorrir mo'r cymod wnaeth Gwenfron a mi.

Mae Gwenfron a minnau yn hen erbyn hyn,
A'r hwyr ar ein pennau fel eira gwyn, gwyn;
Mae'n llygaid yn llwydo fel dydd yn pellhau,
A nerth ein gewynnau o hyd yn gwanhau;
Ond, wele, mae'n cariad o hyd yn cryfhau.
I'r tiroedd dihenaint sy draw tros y lli
Rhyw symud yn dawel wna Gwenfron a mi.

## Gwenfron and I

Gwenfron and I strolled together one day,
As, high in the branches, a breeze laughed away;
A moon shone above, a moon shone in the lake,
A nightingale sang in the valley brake,
Such a night as when love is most wide awake;
And there, as the breeze and the stream murmured by,
We made a firm covenant, Gwenfron and I.

Many years later, when the bare trees below
In the valley were stilled under whitest snow,
The hours of youth had fled evermore,
And everywhere filled with cares by the score,
And the hurricane raged from the woods with a roar.
Be the winter so bitter, let the floods thunder by:
That covenant holds between Gwenfron and I.

Gwenfron and I are agèd by now,
And hoary of head like the whitest snow.
Our eyes are grown dim as the evening light,
Our muscles have wasted, our strength become slight:
But see how our love still increases in might.
To the lands beyond aging we'll go, by and by,
And quietly cross the stream, Gwenfron and I.

## Cri y di-gartref

Af allan i wyneb y ddrycin
 I grwydro hyd lethrau y bryn;
Disgynned y glaw ar fy nillad,
 A chaned y gwynt fel y myn.

Af allan i wyneb y ddrycin,
 'Does undyn yn unman a'm clyw;
'Does neb am oleuo fy llwybyr
 Ond y mellt yn ehangder Duw.

Af allan i wyneb y ddrycin
 Hyd erwau y ddafad a'r oen;
Griddfanned y storm ar fynyddoedd
 Fel darn o ogoniant poen.

Gorwyntoedd gwallgof y bryniau
 Sy'n canu telynau o frwyn,
O cludwch, o cludwch fy ngriddfan
 At rywun a wrendy fy nghŵyn.

\* \* \*

Pan gaeo fy llygaid wrth farw
 Goleued y mellt draws y glyn;
Disgynned y glaw ar fynyddoedd
 A chaned y gwynt fel y myn.

*Pandy, Afon Prysor*

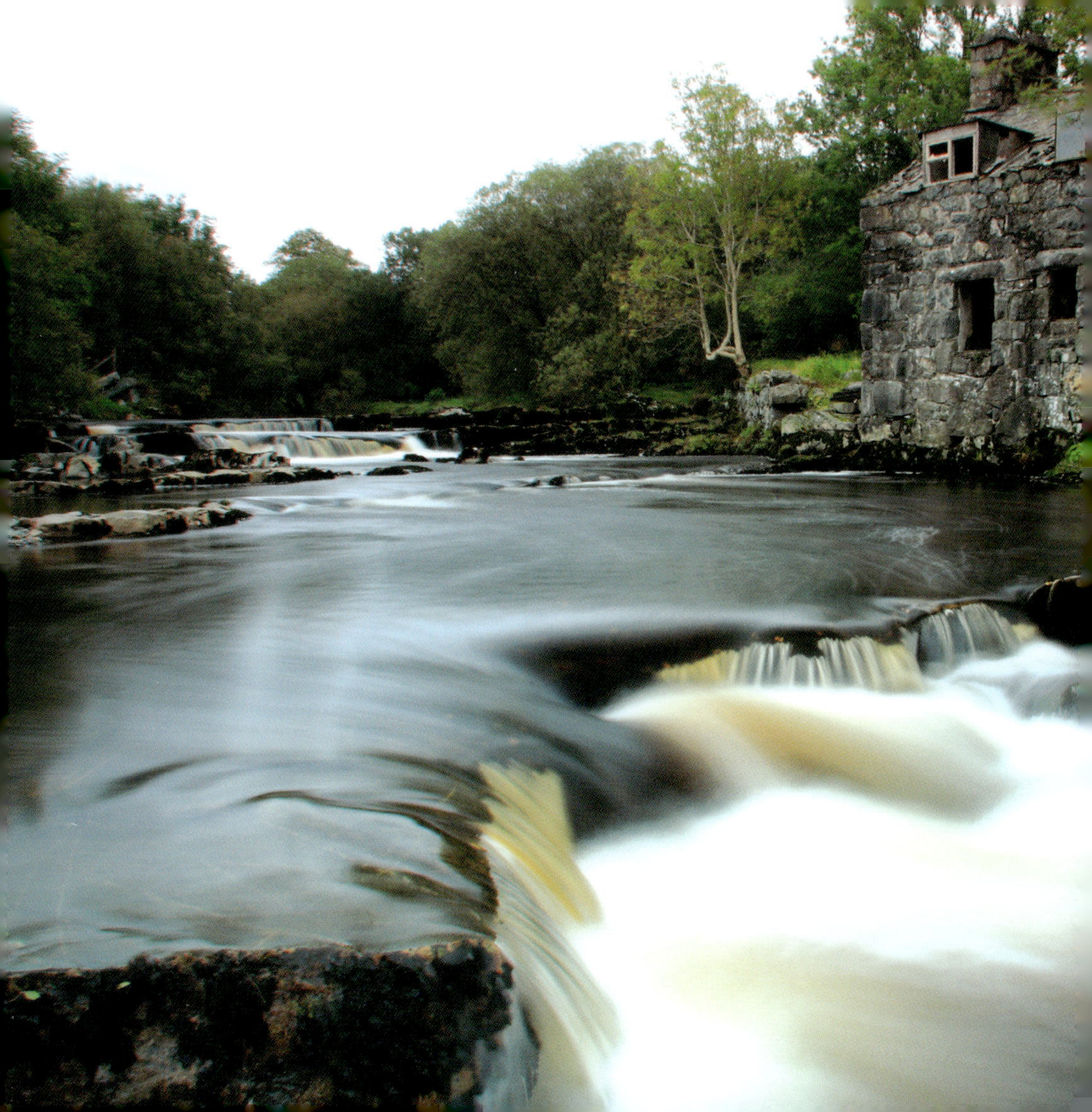

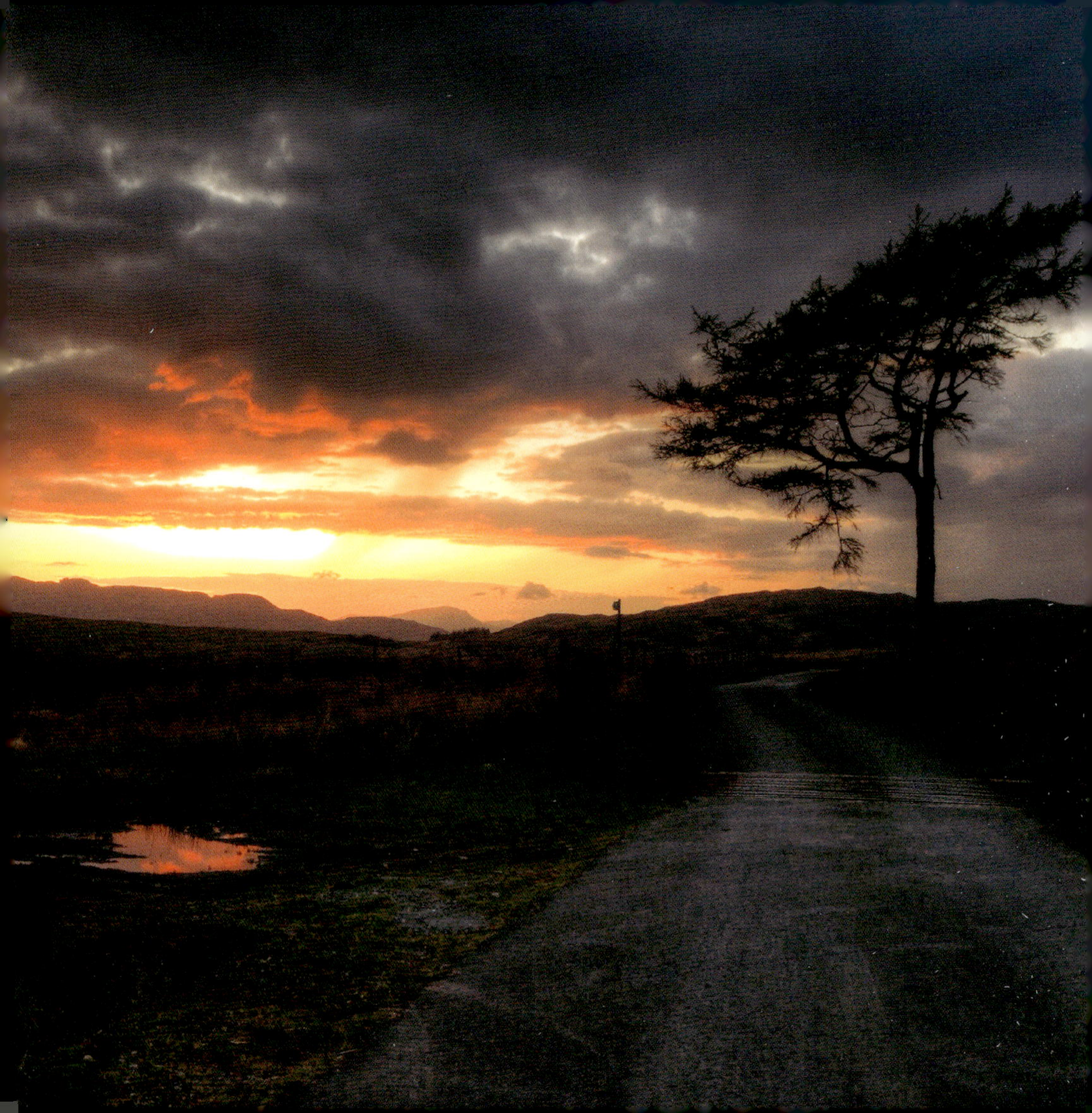

## Facing the tempest

I'll go out in the face of the tempest,
    To wander the slopes of the hill;
Let the deluge rain down on my clothing,
    And let the wind sing as it will.

I'll go out in the face of the tempest,
    No-one anywhere hears my cry;
No-one is going to light my path
    But the lightning of God's immense sky.

I'll go out in the face of the tempest,
    Where the ewe and the lamb roam free,
And let the storm moan in the mountains
    In a glory of agony.

You gales who make harp-strings of rushes,
    Who rage unrestrained in the hills,
Oh carry, oh carry my moaning
    To one who'll give ear to my ills.

\*   \*   \*

When my eyes become closed at my dying,
    Let the deluge rain down on the hill,
Let the lightning flash across the glen,
    And let the wind sing as it will.

*'The Drovers' Tree', Cwm Dôl-gain*

*Hedd Wyn*

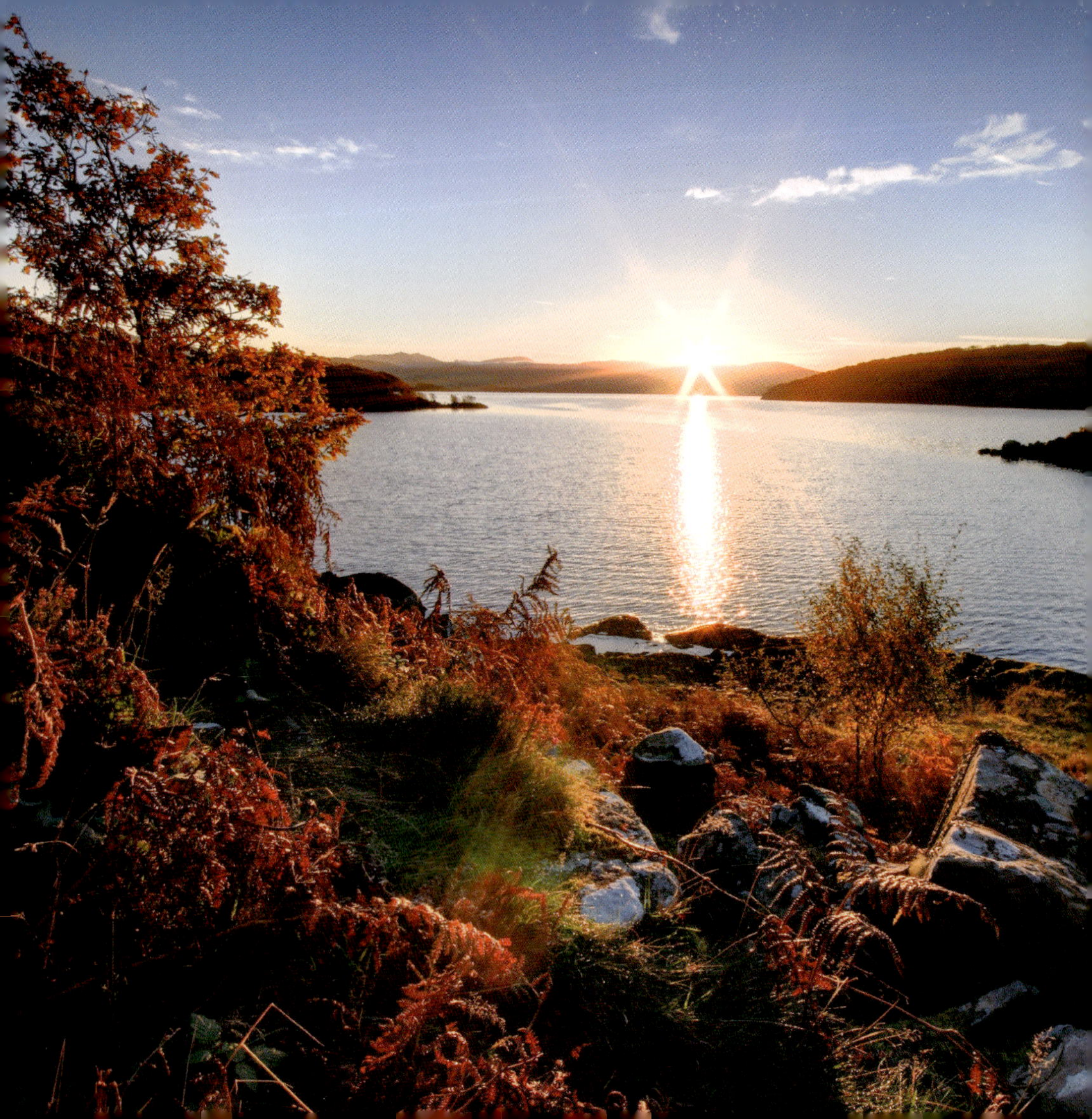

## Claddu mam

Nawnddydd Sadwrn trwy Drawsfynydd
    Cerddai Hydre'n drwm ei droed,
Curai'r gwynt ffenestri'r moelydd,
    Wylai yn y coed.

Pan oedd sŵn y storm yn trydar
    Trwy'r gororau moelion maith,
Cludwyd arch ar ysgwydd pedwar
    Tua'r fynwent laith.

Ond er cludo'r fam i'r graean
    Bydd ei bywyd prydferth gwyn
Megis cân telynau arian
    Fyth ar wynt y glyn.

## A mother's burial

Saturday, and heavy-footed
    Autumn stalked the neighbourhood,
The wind at the windows pelted,
    Wailing in the wood.

As the storm's crescendo sounded
    Through Trawsfynydd's bare surround,
On four shoulders, she was carried
    To the burial ground.

Though the mother now lies buried,
    Her pure virtue lingers there,
As on silver harpstrings sounded
    In the valley air.

*Llyn Trawsfynydd*

*Hedd Wyn*

**Gwladgarwch** (*Detholiadau*)
*Pryddest*

II

Sefais yn oedfa ddilafar y delwau
    Un nawnddydd ar lawnt y dref,
A gelwais i gof rai grwydrodd y ffiniau
A thithau yn farwor ar eu gwefusau
    Pan godent eu gwlatgar lef.

A chlywais wrth gerdded dy fyd hynafol
    Lawer hen faled a chân
Anesid dan angerdd dy chwŷth berorol,
'Sgrifennwyd ar alwad y nwyd anfarwol
    Lefarai o'th golofn dân.

A gwelais wrth gerdded mwsog dy lwybrau
    Gestyll henllwyd a phrudd,
A'r hen dywysogion drengodd ym mrwydrau
Yno yn codi o angof eu beddau
    Yn fanadl a llygaid dydd.

Dyma'r rhai garodd eu henfro a'i hawliau, –
    Wylasant yn nydd ei cham;
Mi wn mai tydi oedd tân eu gwythiennau
A gwn mai tydi arweiniodd eu camrau
    I'w beddau tros wlad eu mam.

**Patriotism** (*Extracts*)
*An Eisteddfod poem*

Canto II

One day in the mute assembly of statues
    On a city square stood I,
Recalling those who wandered the borders
With love of you on their lips like embers
    When they gave patriotic cry.

To my ear, as I walked your world long past,
    Ancient songs and ballads came,
Born in the heat of your musical blast,
Written in immortal passion, and cast
    Forth from your column of flame.

Walking your mossy paths, I saw sullen
    Castles of old, now sunk in gloom;
And warrior princes, long ago fallen
Arose from graves where they lay forgotten
    In bursts of daisies and broom.

*Llyn yr Oerfel, Trawsfynydd*

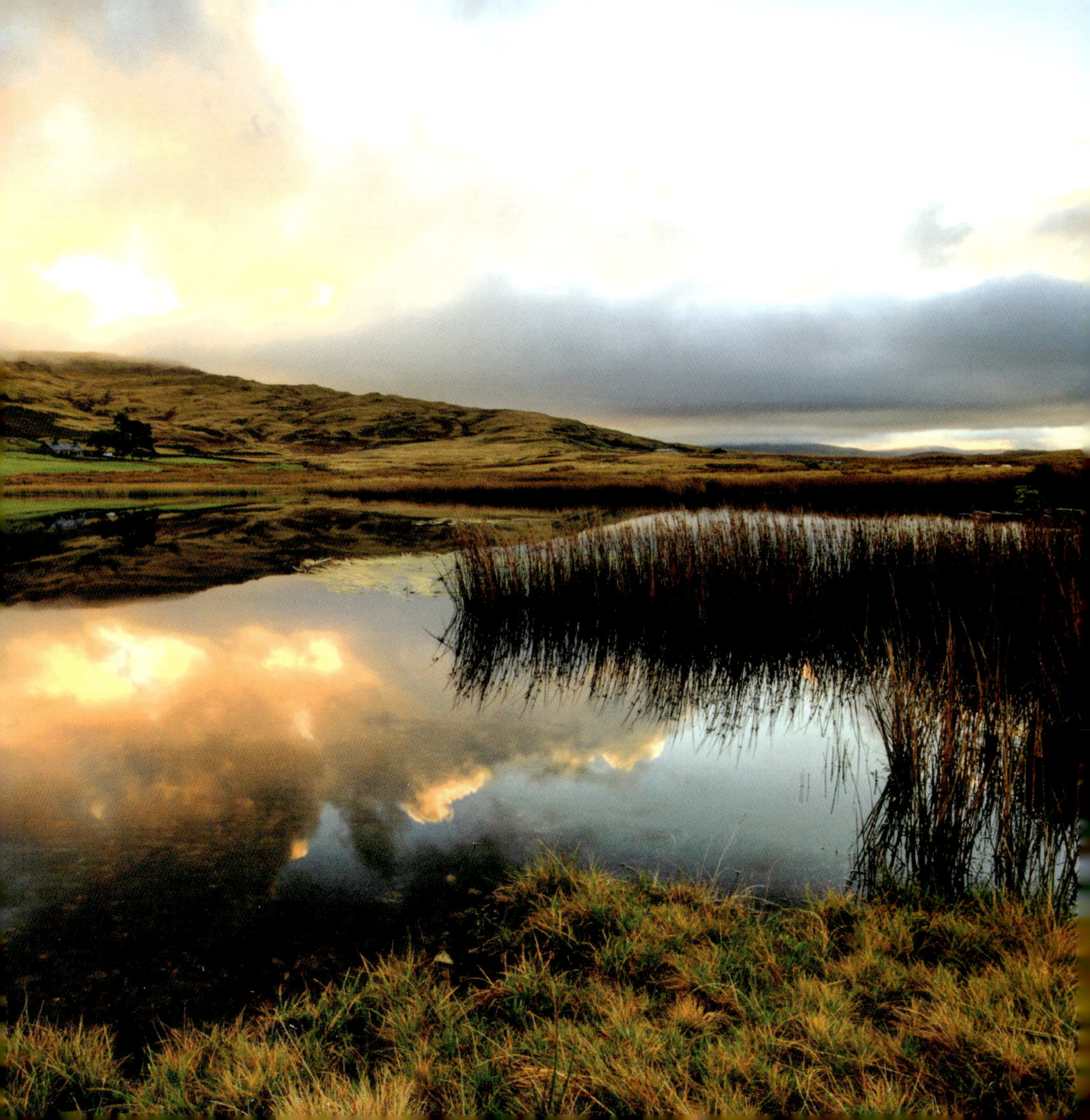

V

Ceni dy delyn am na elli beidio,
    Delynor gobaith dy dud;
Ceni hen gerddi galarus eu hatgo,
Ceni berlesmair breuddwydiol ei deffro
    Ar glybod y llydan fyd.

Lluni delyneg tan dderw y mynydd
    A'i geiriau i gyd yn dân;
Cans onid dy gariad yw bro a nentydd,
Defodau a hawliau dy wlad ddihenydd,
    Ac erddynt ceni dy gân.

Gelwi dy genedl a'r haul ar y bryniau
    I'r "Steddfod" ben bore glân;
A thry pob enaid ym miwsig y tannau
A swyn anfarwol yr hen draddodiadau
    Yn fôr o undeb a chân.

They, who loved their land and its liberties,
    And when it was wronged, they wept;
You, I know, were fire in their arteries,
You also led them to their cemeteries
    When for fatherland they slept.

Canto V

You strike your harp for you cannot refrain,
    Your own nation's hope you sound;
You sing the old songs that recall their pain,
Sing them a dream which awakes them again,
    Sing to the whole wide world.

You shape a lyric where mountain oaks stand,
    And its words are all aflame;
For your love is for streams and heartland,
The rights and claims of your ancient homeland,
    It's for them that you declaim.

Under dawn-lit hills, you call your nation
    All to the festivity;
Each soul now as one in celebration,
To harps and the spell of old tradition
    All in song and unity.

## VI

Eto mae galwad gwladgarwch i'r trinoedd
    Fel yn y dyddiau a fu;
Mae'n alwad yn enw Prydain a'i nerthoedd,
Mae'n alwad yn enw Arglwydd y Lluoedd,
    O'i loew uchelder fry.

Ac wedi yr elo yr heldrin heibio
    Fe ddeffry'r digwmwl ddydd;
Hyd hyn, O Arglwydd, dod lwydd ar ein heiddo
A chadw'n gwladgarwch yn fflam ddiwywo
    Hyd oni ddelom yn rhydd.

## Canto VI

Once more, love of country calls to the fight,
    As it did in days gone by;
Calls in the name of Britain and its might,
In the name of the Lord of Hosts, from bright
    Heaven up above on high.

And then, when the fighting is all over,
    Then will day dawn cloudlessly;
For now, O Lord, grant that we may prosper,
And keep the flame of patriotic fervour
    Unfading until we're free.

## Marw yn ieuanc

Bu farw yn ieuanc, a'r hafddydd
    Yn crwydro ar ddôl, ac ar fryn:
Aeth ymaith i'r tiroedd tragywydd
    Fel deilen ar wyntoedd y glyn.

Hi garodd gynefin bugeiliaid
    A chwmni'r mynyddoedd maith, mawr;
A llanw meddyliau ei henaid
    Wnâi miwsig yr awel a'r wawr.

Bu fyw yn ddirodres a thawel,
    Yn brydferth, yn bur, ac yn lân;
Ac eto mor syml â'r awel
    Sy'n canu trwy'r cymoedd ei chân.

Fe'i magwyd ym murmur y nentydd
    Ar fryniau diarffordd Tŵr Maen;
Nid rhyfedd i'w bywyd ysblennydd
    Flaguro mor bur a di-staen.

Mor ddiwyd oedd hi gyda'i gorchwyl,
    Mor drylwyr cyflawnai ei gwaith –
'Roedd delw gonestrwydd dinoswyl
    Yn llanw ei bywyd di-graith;

Bu farw yn nyddiau ieuenctyd
    A'i heinioes ar hanner ei byw;
Bu farw a'r haf yn ei bywyd,
    Bu farw yn blentyn i Dduw.

Fe'i gwelsom hi'n gwywo i'r beddrod
    A'i haul tros y ffin yn pellhau;
A hithau, y Nefoedd ddiddarfod,
    I'w chyfwrdd i'r glyn yn nesáu.

Daw atgof ei bywyd a'i geiriau
    Yn ôl i'n calonnau fel cynt,
Fel arogl mil myrdd o lilïau,
Fel miwsig perorol o glychau
    Y nefoedd, ar lanw y gwynt.

*Above Trawsfynydd*

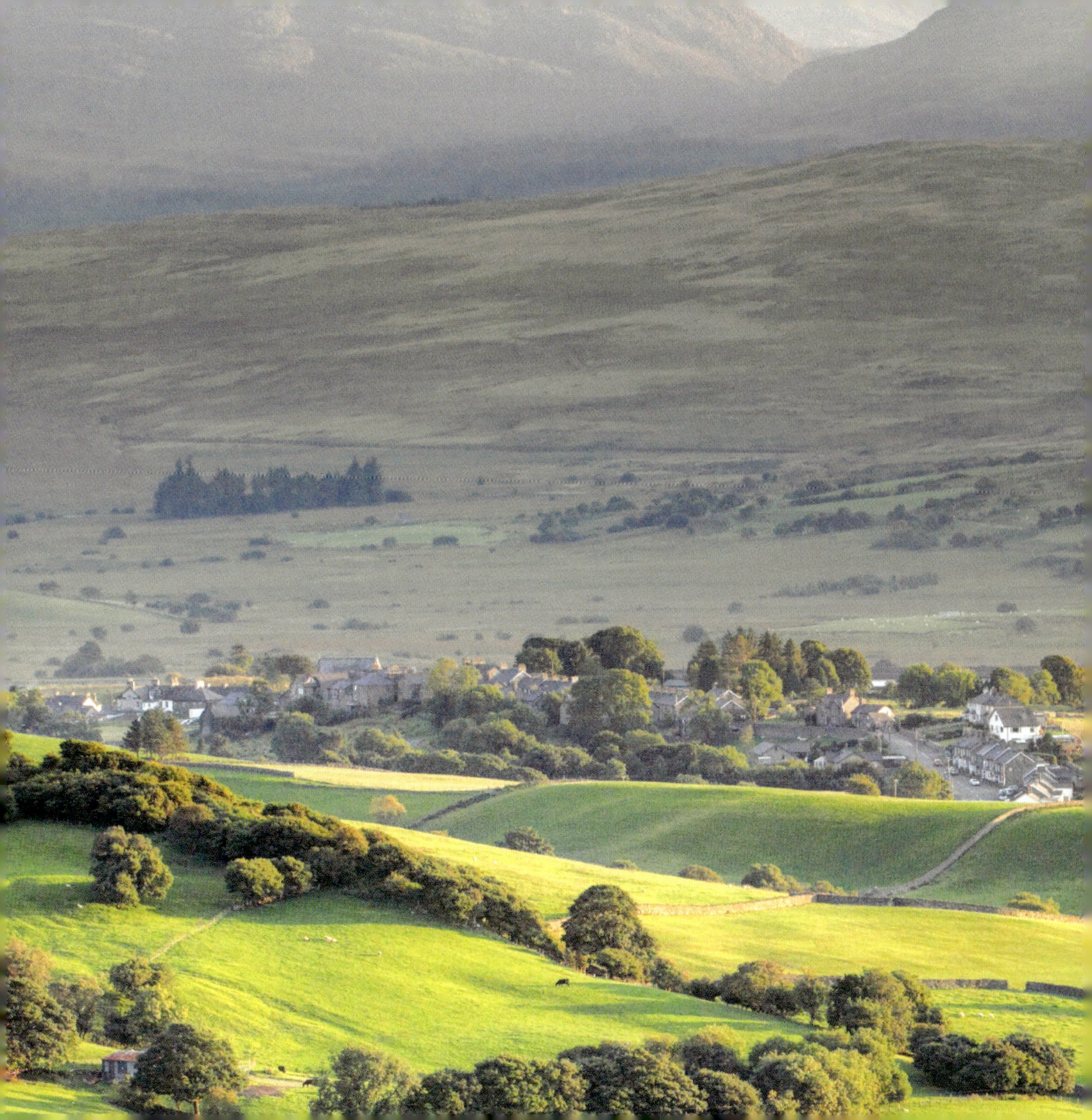

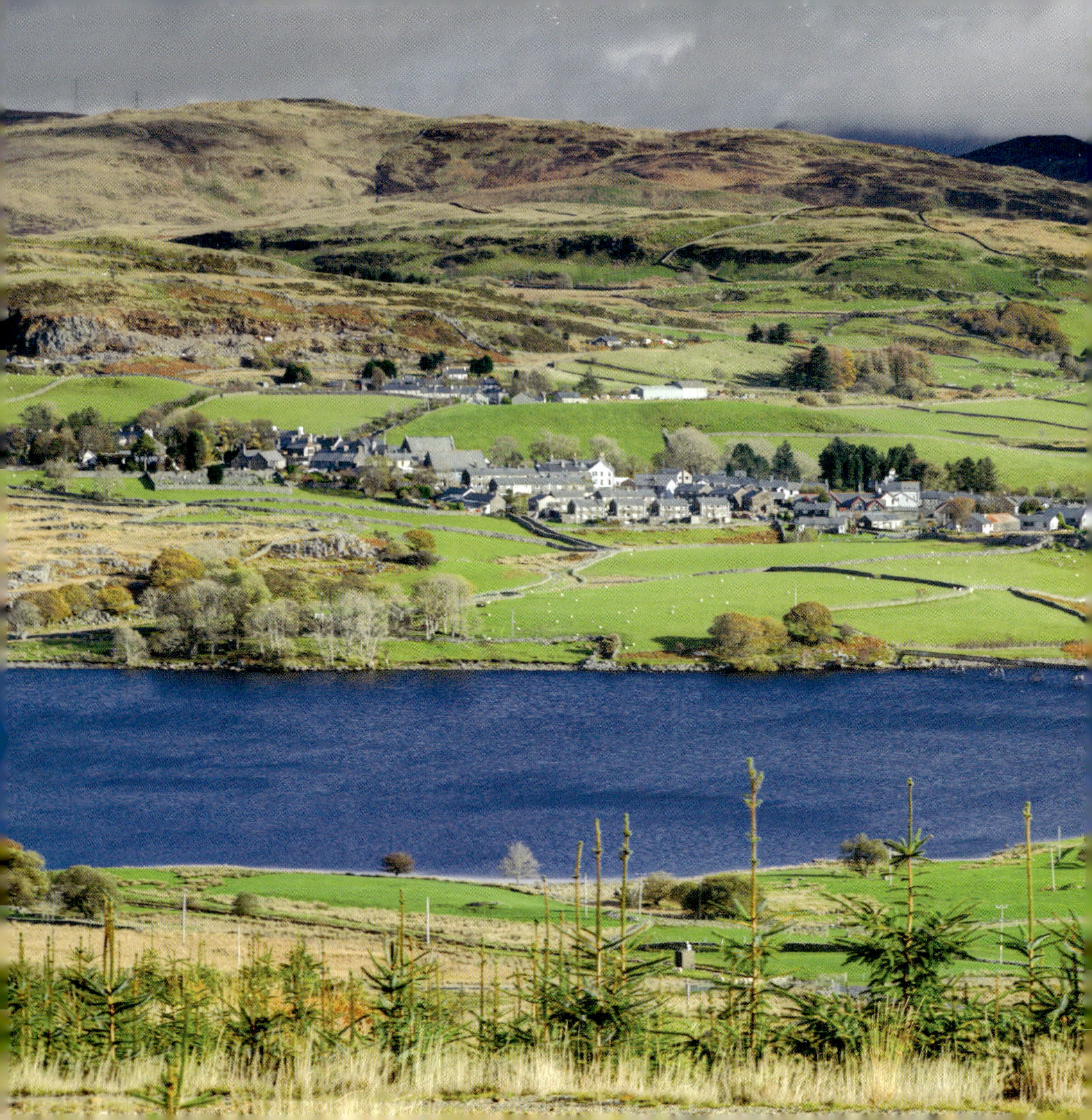

## To die young

She died young, when on hill and meadow
    The Summer comes wandering fair,
She set out for the eternal lands
    Like a leaf on the valley's air.

She loved the company of peaks,
    The pastures where shepherds stray,
Where the music of the breeze
    Filled her soul at break of day.

She led a beautiful, pure, clean life
    In quiet and sincerity,
And yet as simple as the breeze
    Which sings through the valleys was she.

She was raised to the music of mountain streams
    On the hills of Twr Maen so remote;
Small wonder that her splendid life
    Budded forth without stain or mote.

So industrious was she at her duties,
    Completing her work through and through,
The image of ceaseless honesty
    Filled her life of immaculate hue.

She died in the days of maidenhood,
    Her mortal span but half-spent;
She died as one who's a child of God,
    And at the height of her summertime,
                              went.

With her sun setting into the grave
    We watched her decline and fail
As the eternal Heavens approached
    To meet her down in the vale.

Her words and her life for ever more
    In our hearts, as before, will dwell,
Like the scent of a myriad lilies, or
A peal of heavenly bells, as they pour
    Their sound on the breeze's swell.

*Trawsfynydd from across the lake*

*Hedd Wyn*

### Dymuniad

Dymunwn fod yn flodyn – a'r awel
Garuaidd yn disgyn
Arnaf i yn genlli gwyn
Oddi ar foelydd eurfelyn.


### A wish

I'd wish to be a flower – and caressed
By a breeze so tender
From golden hills, to confer
On me a shining shower.

*Plu'r gweunydd (cotton-grass) and Manod Mawr*

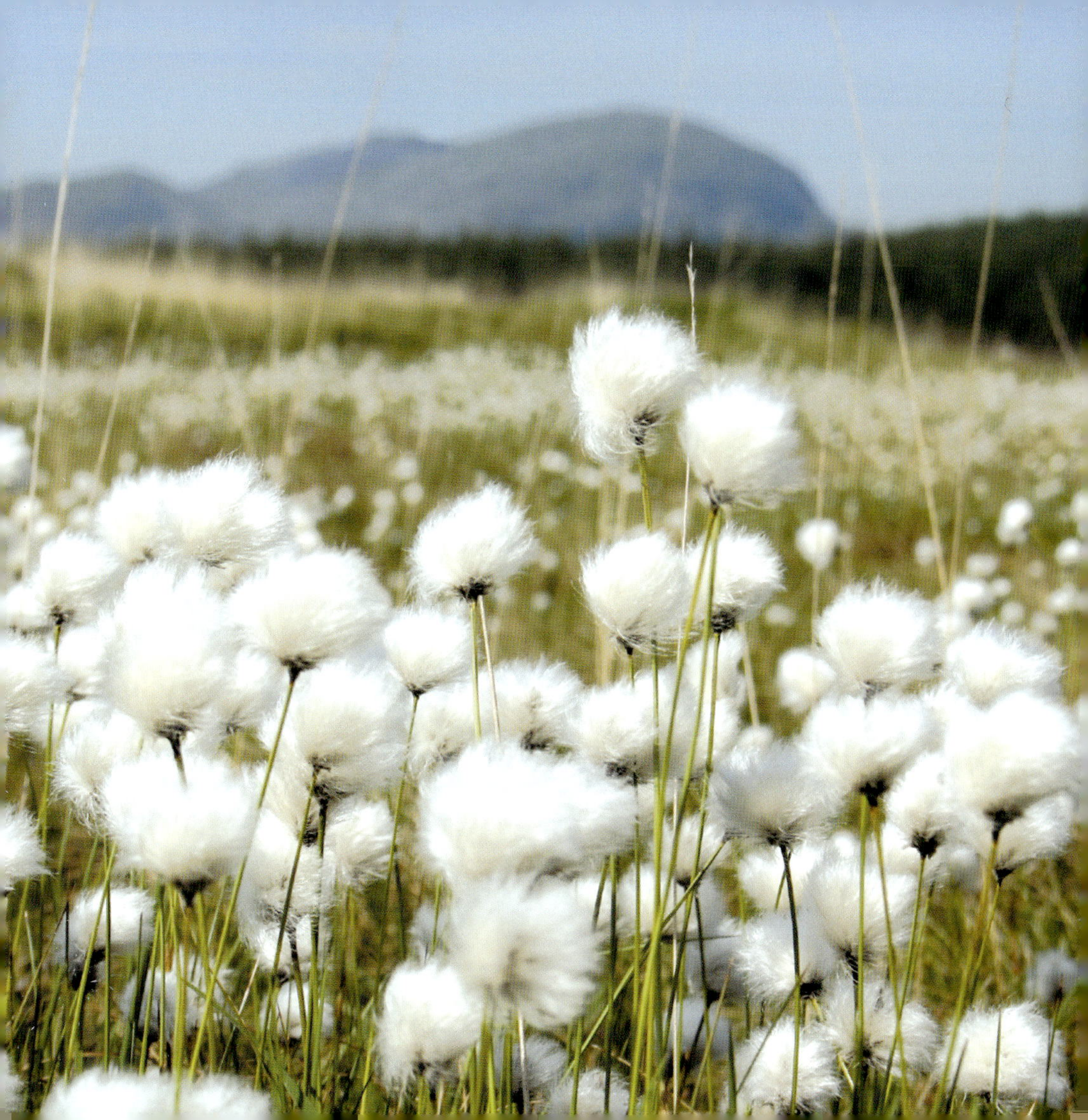

**Y wawr**

Hi gwyd o gwsg oed o gân – hithau'r nos
O'i thrô'n niwl dry allan;
A gwêl ar oriel arian
Drem y dydd fel drama dân.

## The dawn

She arises to singing – and compels
Misty night's dethroning;
On silver heights, she sees fire bring
The drama of day's coming.

*The sun rising behind Yr Ysgwrn*

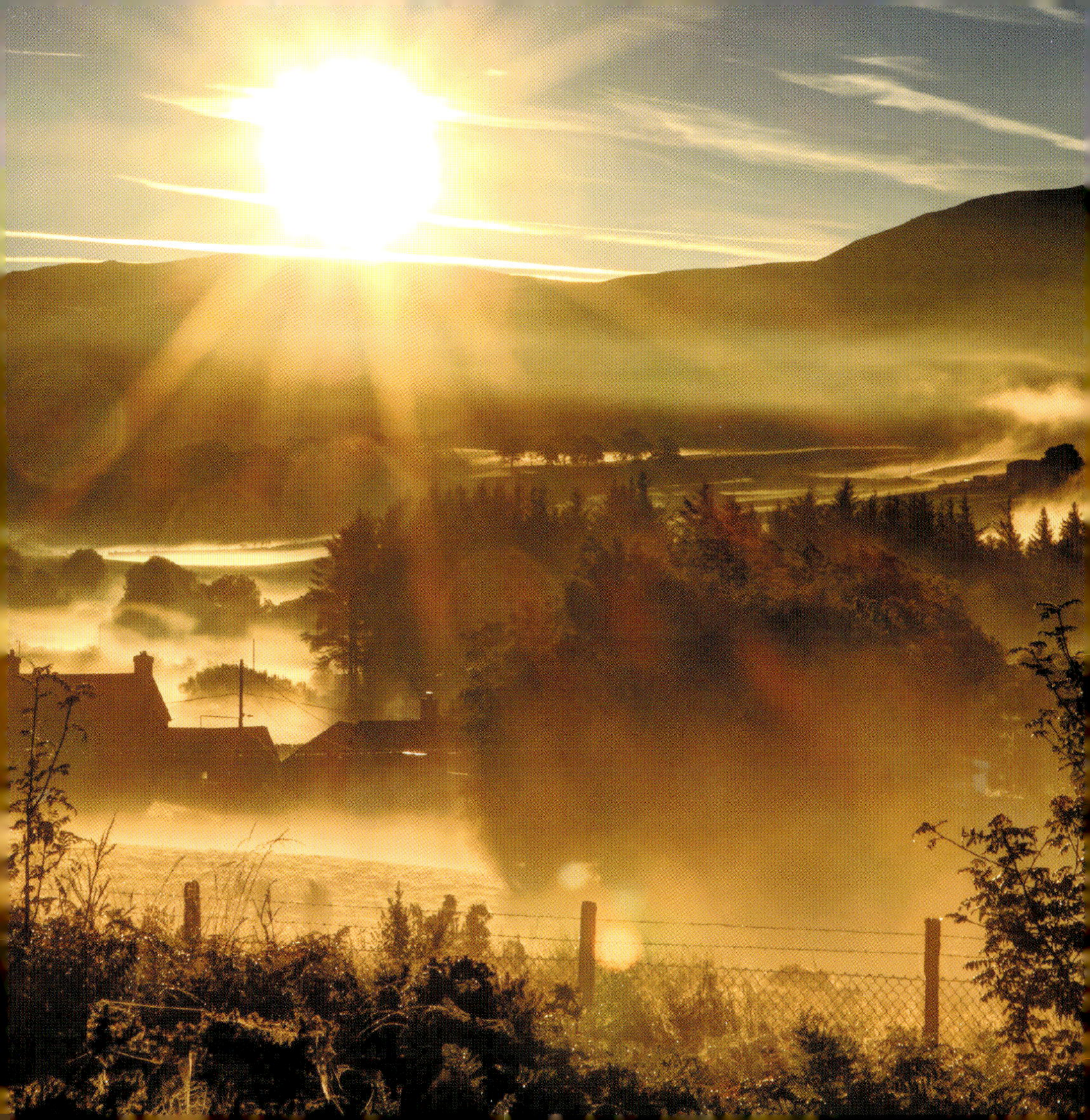

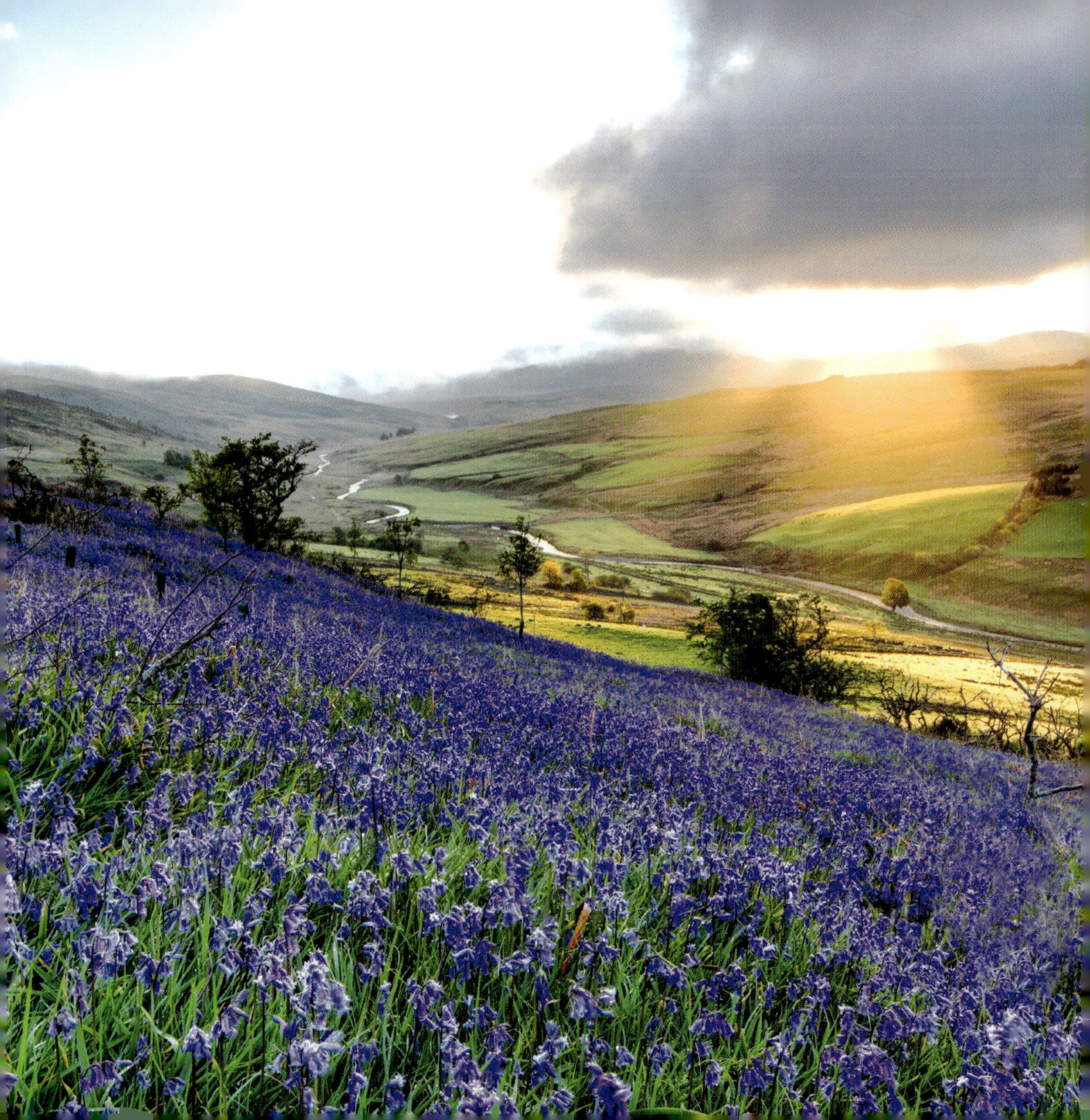

## Haul ar fynydd

Cerddais fin pêr aberoedd – yn nhwrf swil
Nerfus wynt y ffriddoedd;
A braich wen yr heulwen oedd
Am hen wddw'r mynyddoedd.


## The sun on the mountain

By sweet streams I went walking – as the shy
Moorland breeze was playing;
And pale sunshine's arm did cling
To the old hills, embracing.

*Bluebells, Cwm Dôl-gain*

*Hedd Wyn*

### Y Moelwyn

Oer ei drum, garw'i dremynt – yw erioed,
    A'i rug iddo'n emrynt;
  Iach oror praidd a cherrynt
  A'i greigiau'n organau'r gwynt.

## Y Moelwyn

Ever cold, and rough its brows – where the flocks
    Roam its heathery furrows;
  An organ, as the high wind blows
  Howling in rocky hollows.

*Moelwynion from Trawsfynydd*

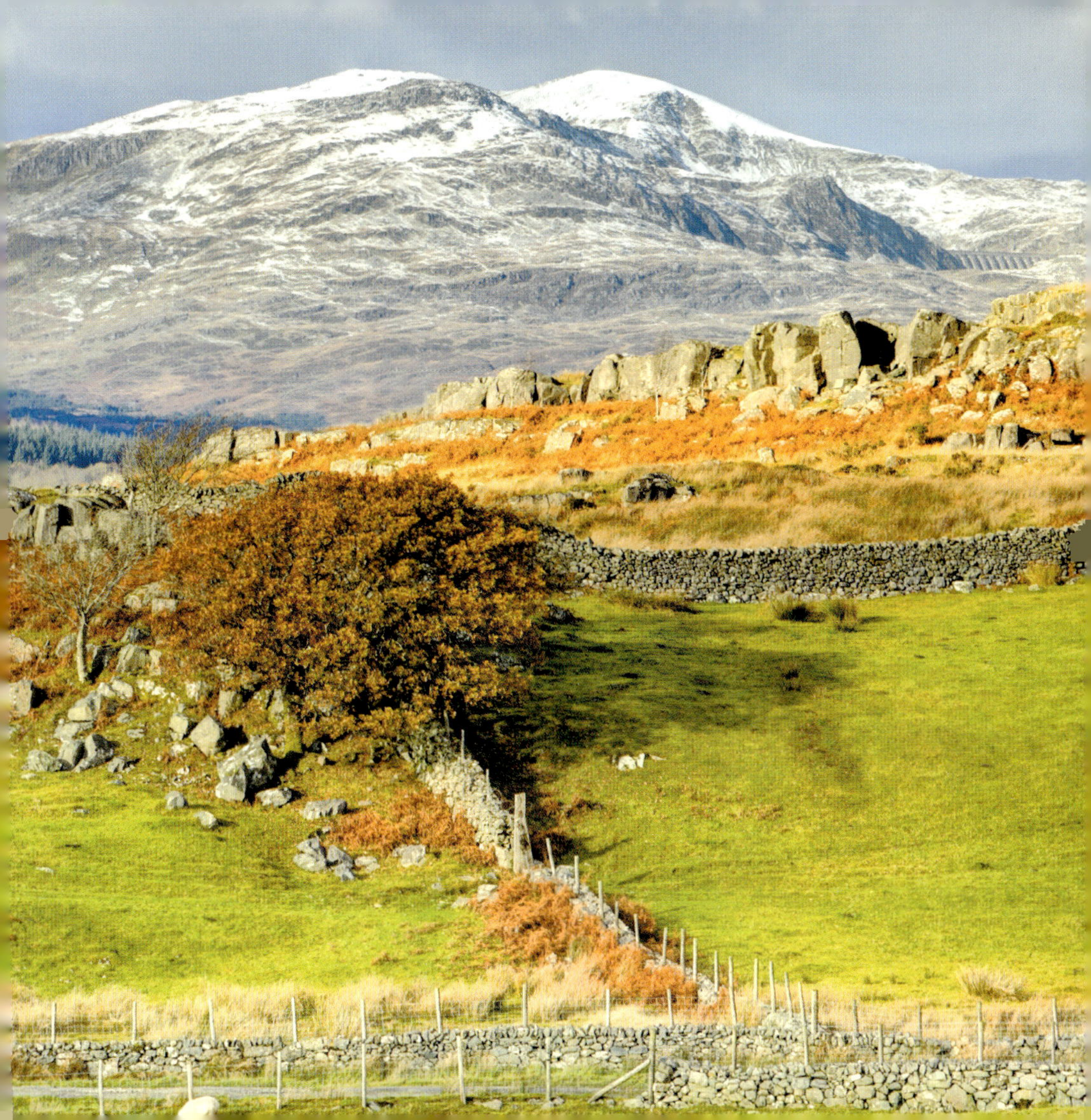

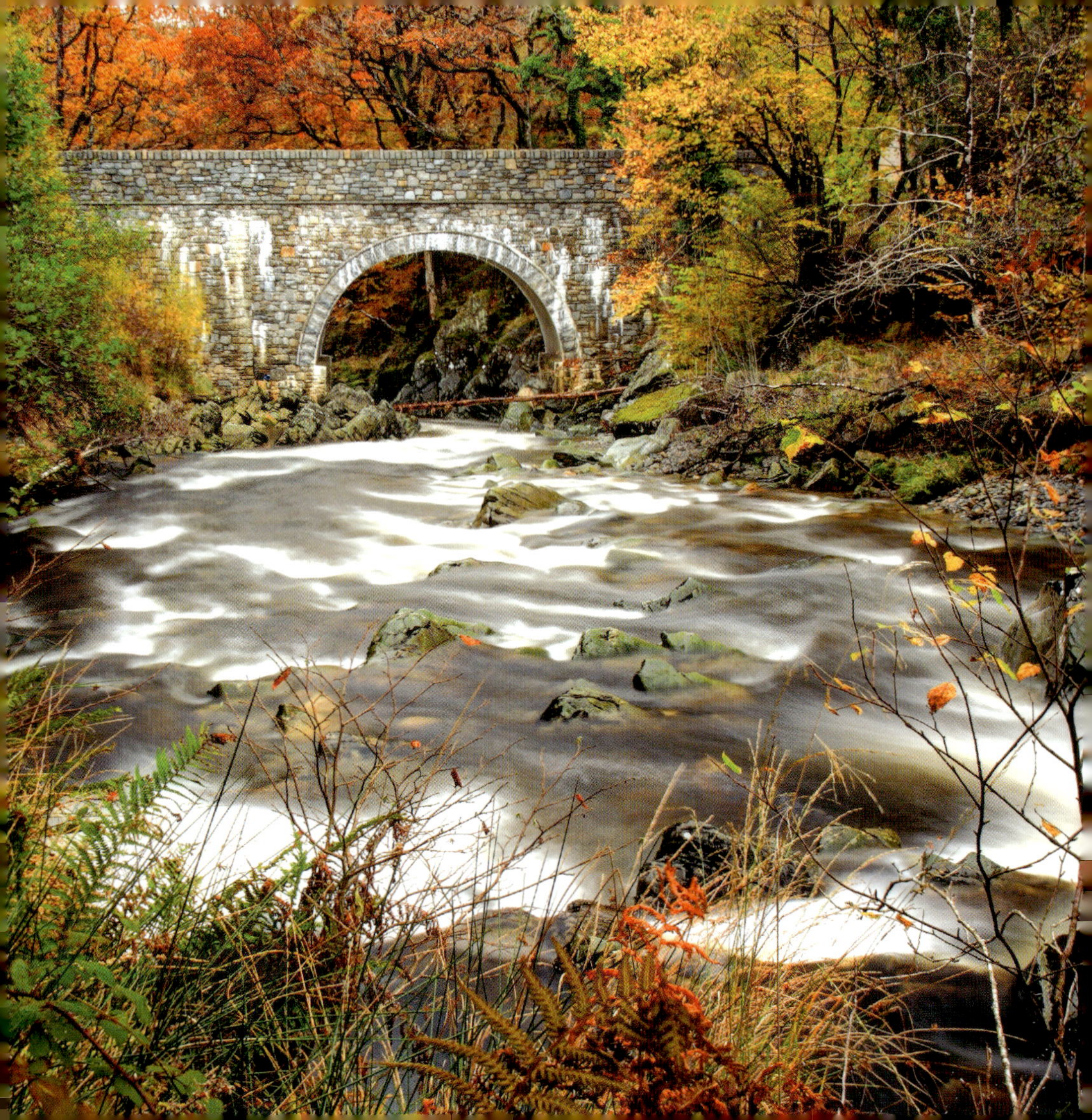

### Llwybrau'r drin

Ewrob sy acw'r awran – dan ei gwaed
    Yn y gwynt yn griddfan;
    Malurir ei themlau eirian
A'i herwau teg sy'n galendr tân.

## The paths of war

Behold Europe at present – all bloodied,
    Groaning, its resplendent
    Temples by the tempest rent,
Fair lands in fiery torment.

*Pont Rhyd y Dail*

*Hedd Wyn*

## Gwersyll Litherland

Gwêl wastad hutiau'n glwstwr – a bechgyn
 Bochgoch yn llawn dwndwr;
O'u gweld fe ddywed pob gŵr:
Dyma aelwyd y milwr.


## Litherland Camp

Behold huts in a cluster – and red-cheeked
 Boys in all their thunder;
To see them, all would aver:
This is the soldiers' quarter.

**Priodas ddydd y rhyfel**

Er dur wae y brwydro erch – hwyliasant
I lysoedd gwyn traserch;
Yno mae pob rhyw lannerch
Yn rosyns aur a swyn serch!

# A marriage in wartime

Despite war's woe and torment – they've entered
Love's courts of endearment,
There the golden roses scent
Each grove with sweet enchantment!

*Hedd Wyn*

## I Blant Trawsfynydd ar Wasgar, 1914

Holi'n wan amdanoch – fore a hwyr
    Mae y fro adawsoch;
  Yntau y cryf gorwynt croch
  Eto sy'n cofio atoch.

Er oedi'n wasgaredig – hyd erwau
    Y tiroedd pellennig,
  Duw o'i ras a lanwo'ch trig
  Â dialar Nadolig.

Rhai o'r hen bererinion, – oedd unwaith
    Yn ddiddanwch Seion,
  Aethant o'n hardal weithion
  I'r wlad well dros feryl don.

Eraill aeth dros y gorwel – i feysydd
    Difiwsig y rhyfel;
  Uwch eu cad boed llewych cêl
  Adenydd y Duw anwel.

Rhai ohonoch geir heno – hwnt y môr
    Glasfant maith sy'n cwyno;
  Efo'r gwynt tros ei frig o
  Caf hiraeth yn cyfeirio.

Draw i afiaith y trefydd, – llu eraill
    A yrrwyd o'n bröydd;
  Uwch eu llwyd hen aelwydydd
  Acen salm y ddrycin sydd.

Er hynny, bell garennydd, – un ydyw'n
    Dymuniadau beunydd;
  Ni all pellter Iwerydd
  Lwydo'r hen deimladau rhydd.

Er y siom trwy'r henfro sydd, – a'r adwyth
    Ddifroda'n haelwydydd;
  Hwyrach y daw cliriach dydd
  Tros fannau hoff Trawsfynydd.

*Hafod Wen, Cwm Prysor*

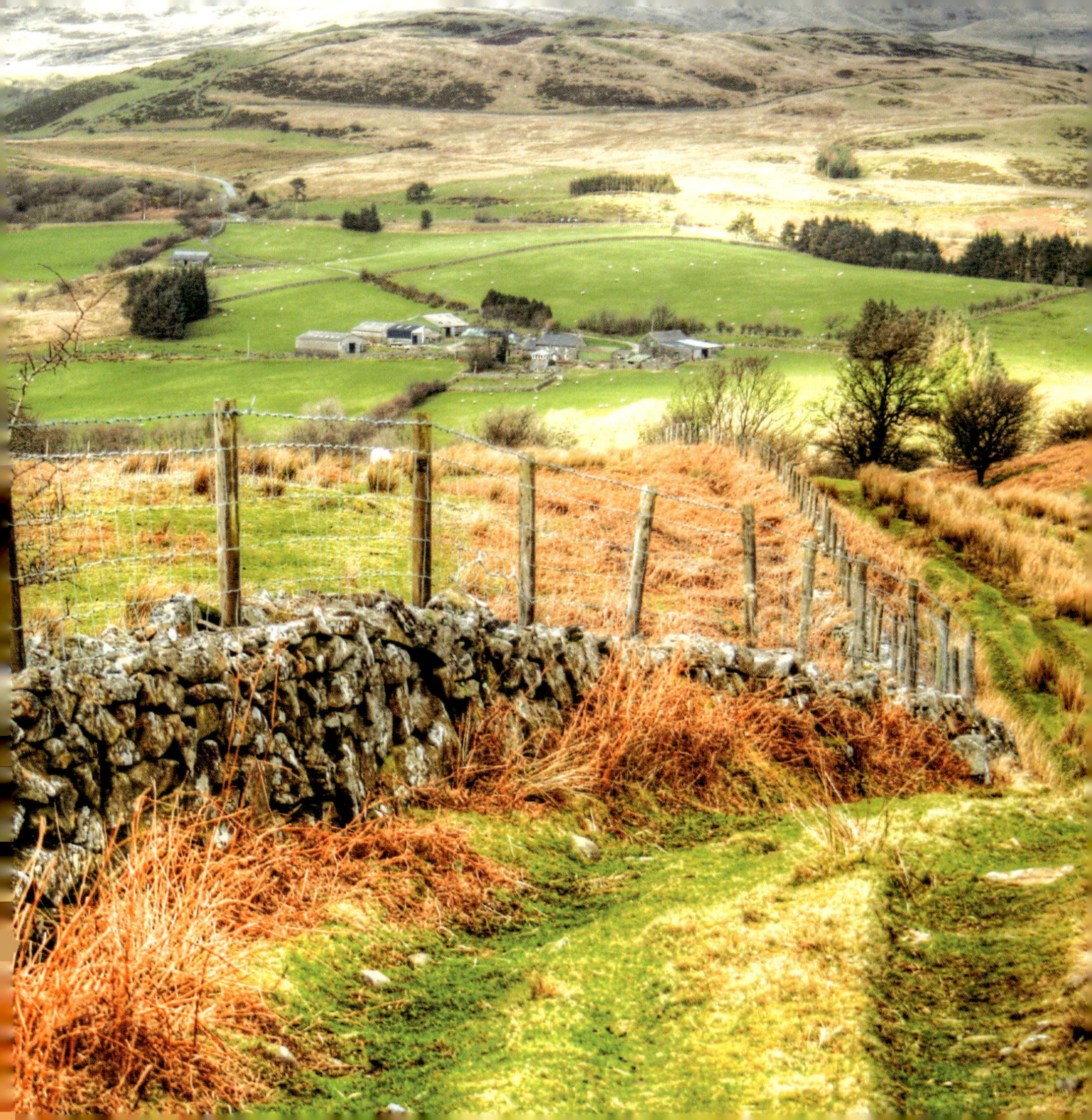

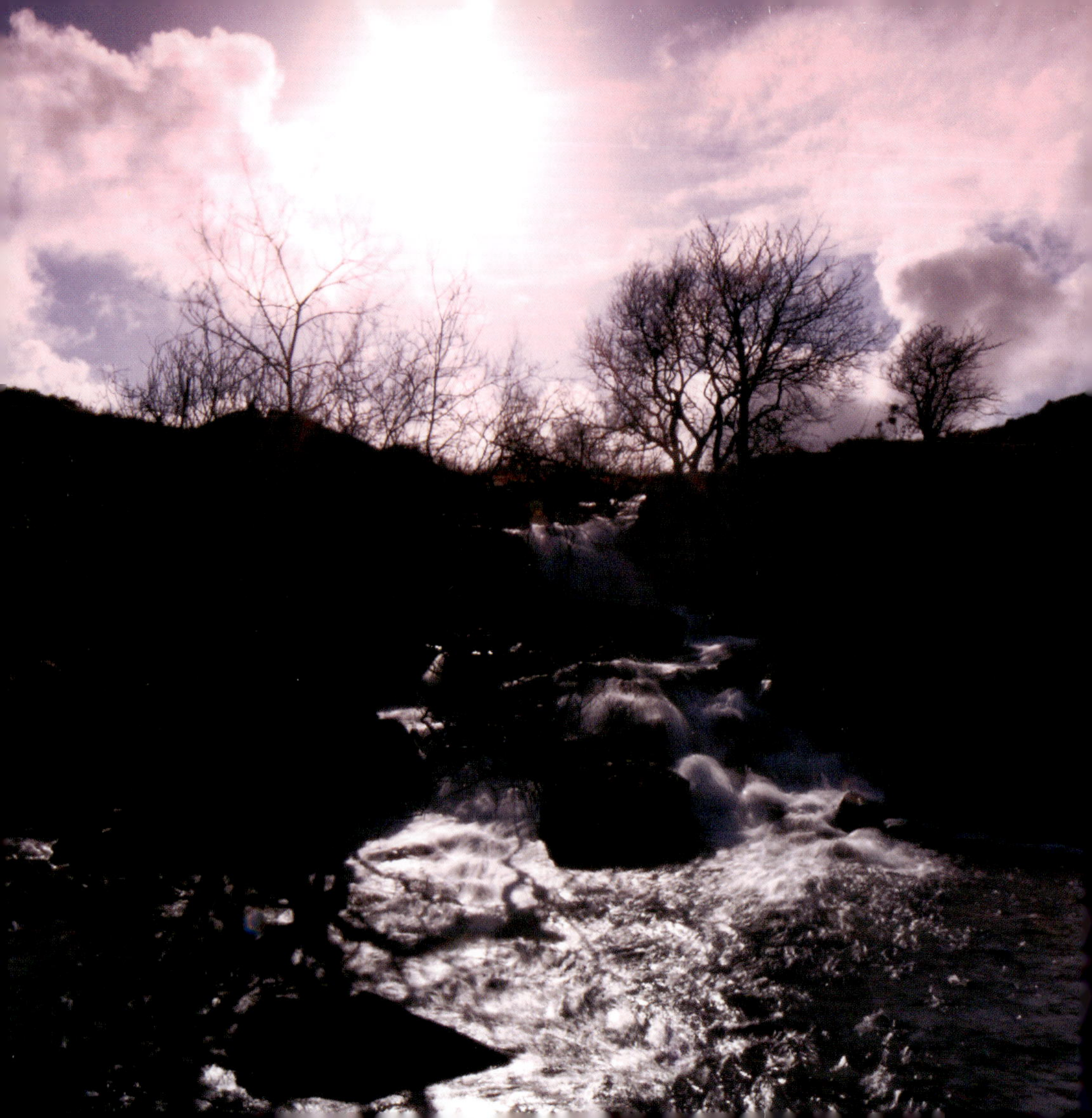

# To the scattered children of Trawsfynydd, 1914

Day and night, the home country – that you left
    Asks about you feebly;
  The raging hurricane, he
  Sends his regards most loudly.

Though you delay in staying – yet in those
    Acres of your sowing
  Far and wide, may God's grace bring
  Glad Noël to your dwelling.

Some of the old have passed on – pilgrims who
    Once delighted Zion;
  Over beryl waves they've gone
  To find a better mansion.

Others crossed the horizon – to fields where
    War sounds in confusion;
  Overhead, as they fight on,
  God's wings be their protection.

Some of you, this evening – are beyond
    That blue void, the grumbling
  Sea; above, the wind takes wing
  And bears to you our longing.

Others from our homelands sent – far away
    To the cities' ferment;
  Above their hearths sounds the lament
  Sung by the storm in torment.

For all that, distant kinsmen – our daily
    Regards flow unbroken;
  All the wide Atlantic's span
  Can't pall the old emotion.

Despite our disillusion – and the blight
    Of our hearths' destruction,
  One day we may see the sun
  And Trawsfynydd's hills brighten.

*Rhaeadr Llewyrch, Llyn Trawsfynydd*

*Hedd Wyn*

## Plant Trawsfynydd, 1915

Pe doech yn ôl i fro eich cydnabod,
    Chwi welech fel cynt
Eira fel llynges dlos o wylanod
    Ar lanw y gwynt.

Gwelech lwydni y gaeaf diwenau
    Ar fynydd a rhos;
Clywech y corwynt fel storm o dduwiau
    Yng nghanol y nos.

Yma mae celloedd gwag dan y ddrycin
    Yn fud a di-fri,
A'r gwynt yn chwilio pob llofft a chegin
    Amdanoch chwi.

Pell yw'r ieuenctid llawen eu dwndwr
    Fu'n cerdded y fro;
'Chydig sy'n mynd at y Bont a'r Merddwr
    Yn awr ar eu tro.

Holi amdanoch â llais clwyfedig
    Mae'r ardal i gyd;
Chwithau ymhell fel dail gwasgaredig
    Ar chwâl tros y byd.

Rhai ohonoch sy 'merw y brwydrau
    Yn y rhyfel draw,
A sŵn diorffwys myrdd o fagnelau
    O'ch cylch yn ddi-daw.

Eraill sy'n crwydro gwledydd pellennig
    Yn alltud eu hynt
Ac yn eu calon atgo Nadolig
    Yr hen ardal gynt.

P'le bynnag yr ydych, blant Trawsfynydd,
    Ar ledled y byd,
Gartre mae rhywrai ar eu haelwydydd
    Yn eich cofio i gyd.

Ni all pellterau eich gyrru yn ango,
    Blant y bryniau glân;
Calon wrth galon sy'n aros eto,
    Er ar wahân.

A phan ddaw gŵyl y Nadolig heibio
    I'r ddaear i gyd,
Blant Trawsfynydd, tan arfau neu beidio,
    Gwyn fo eich byd.

\*   \*   \*

# The children of Trawsfynydd, 1915

If you returned, you'd see here in
    The land you know,
Snow like a pretty fleet of gulls
    On the wind's flow.

You'd see on hill and moor unsmiling
    Winter's blight,
You'd hear a storm like the gods' ire
    At dead of night.

Here beneath the gale lie homesteads
    Mute and stricken,
Searching for you, the wind blows
    Through loft and kitchen.

Far are the happy, noisy youths
    Who strolled this quarter,
Few are those who now frequent
    The bridge and water.

Broken-voiced, all here are asking
    How you are,
You, like leaves across the world
    Scattered afar.

Some of you are distant in
    The thick of war,
All around, a thousand guns
    Ceaselessly roar.

\*   \*   \*

Others in far countries now
    As exiles roam,
And in their hearts, remembering
    Christmas at home.

Oh, children of Trawsfynydd, throughout
    All the earth,
Back home, somebody thinks of you
    At every hearth.

Children of the hills, though far,
    You're not forgotten;
Though separated, heart from heart
    Remains unriven.

When Christmas comes to all the earth,
    Trawsfynydd's seed,
Whether armed or not, may you be
    Blessed indeed.

*Hedd Wyn*

**Blodau Coffa**

**Marw un fach**

Gwenodd uwch ei theganau – am ennyd
Mewn mwyniant digroesau;
Heddiw ceir uwch ei bedd cau
Efengyl chwerwaf angau.

# Memorial Flowers

### The death of a little girl

With joy, her toys she'd treasure – for a while
With such carefree pleasure;
Today death writes upon her
Headstone, a truth so bitter.

*Rhinogydd from Cwm Dôl-gain*

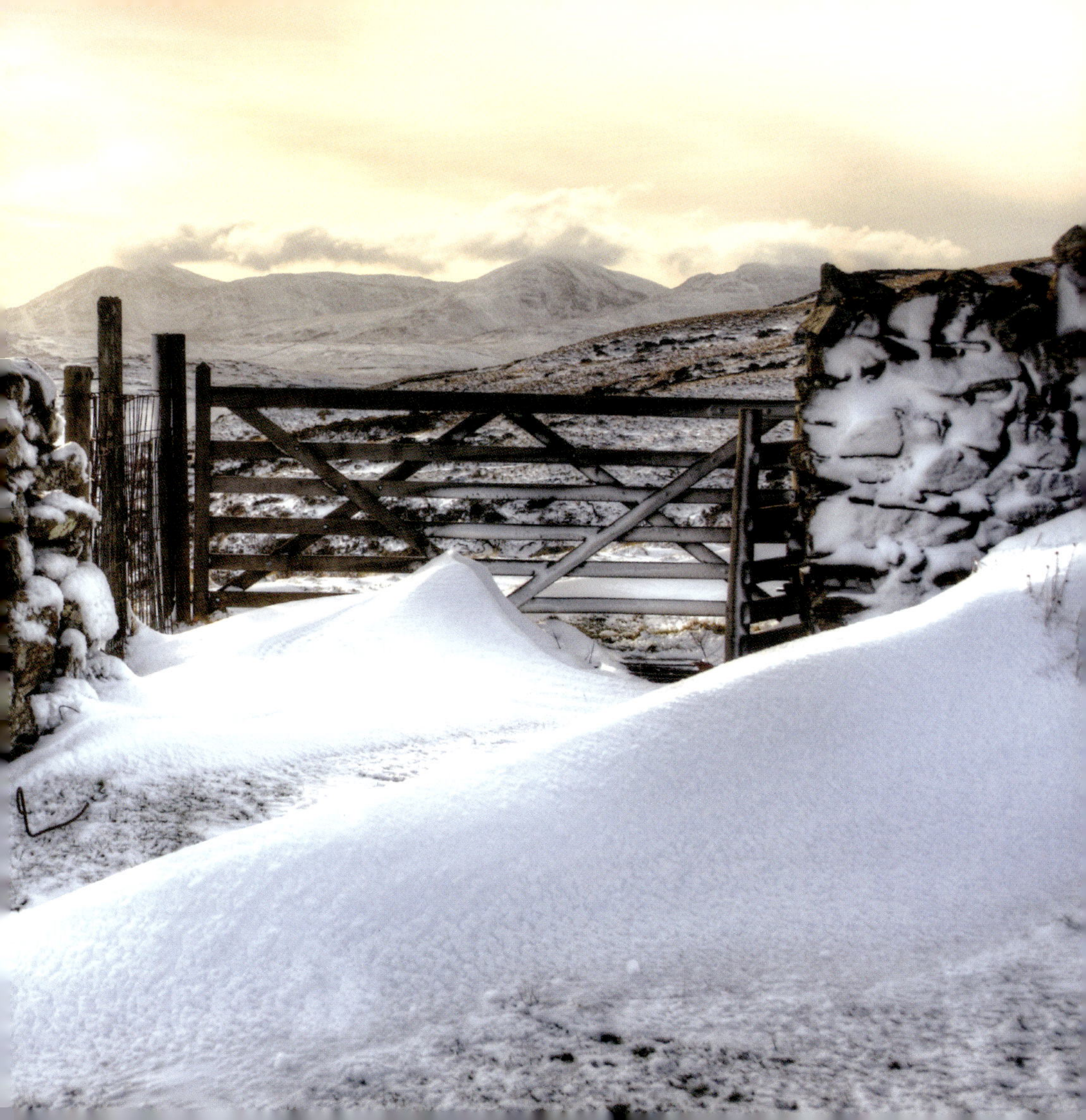

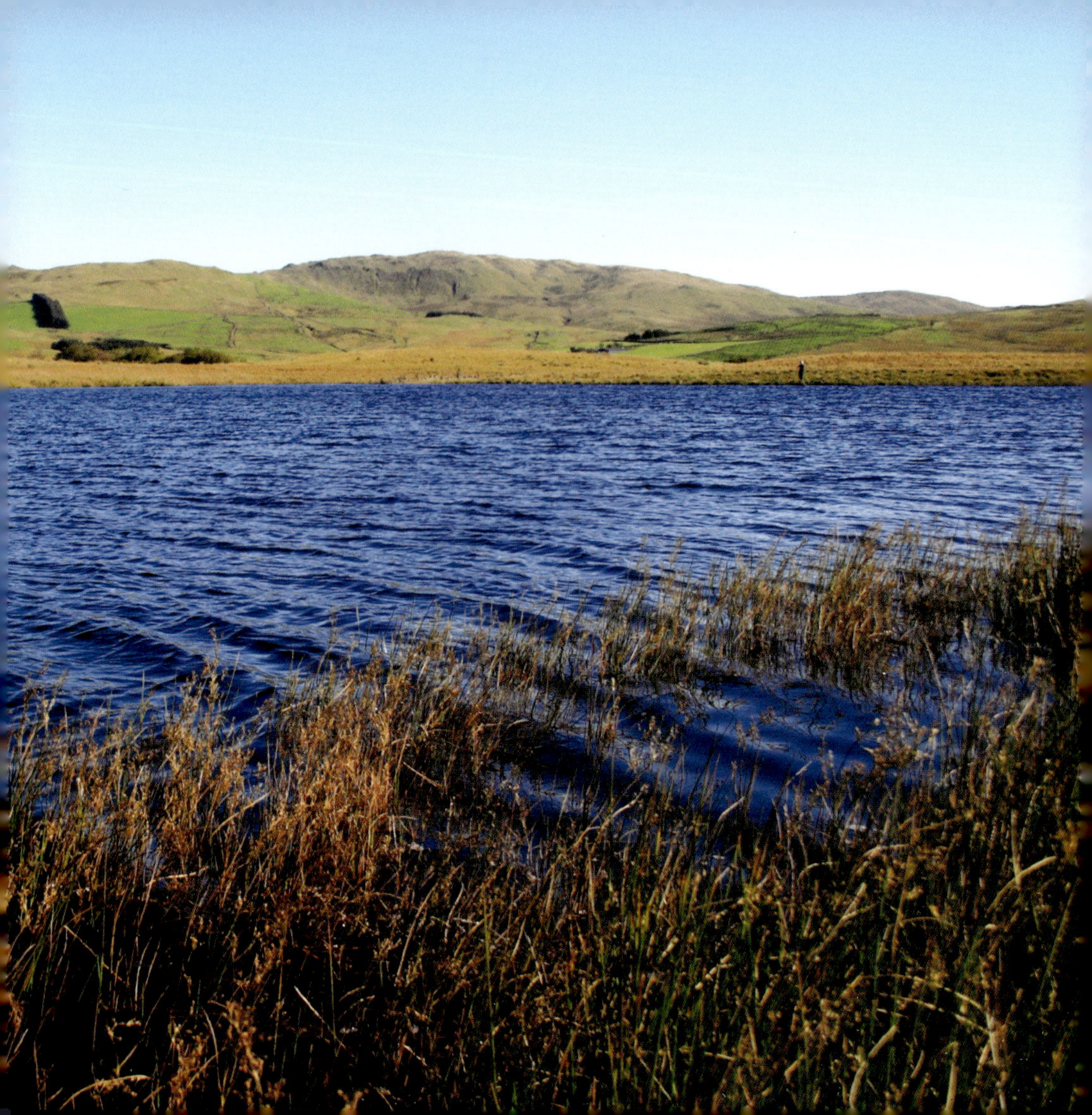

## Griff Llewelyn

Y llynedd mi welais Griffith Llewelyn,
Ei lygaid yn lasliw, ei wallt yn felyn.

Yn ei olwg lednais a'i dremiad tawel
'Roedd nodau ei deulu, a golau'r capel.

Ond heddiw mae'i deulu o dan y cymyl,
Ac yntau yn huno yn sŵn y megnyl.

Caethiwa di, Arglwydd, ddwylo y gelyn
Darawodd un annwyl fel Griff Llewelyn.

## Griff Llewelyn

Griffith Llewelyn I saw last year,
His hair was yellow, his eyes azure.

On his modest demeanour was his family's stamp,
In his quiet gaze shone the chapel lamp.

But today sees his family under a cloud,
As he lies asleep where the guns roar loud.

Bind Thou, O Lord, the hands of the foe
Who laid dear Griffith Llewelyn low.

*Hiraethlyn*

*Hedd Wyn*

**Nid â'n ango**

Ei aberth nid â heibio, – ei wyneb
Annwyl nid â'n ango,
Er i'r Almaen ystaenio
Ei dwrn dur yn ei waed o.


# Unforgotten

His sacrifice abided – his dear face
Ever recollected,
Though Germany has tinted
Her iron fist a bloody red.

*Bryn y Gofeb (memorial cross, Trawsfynydd)*

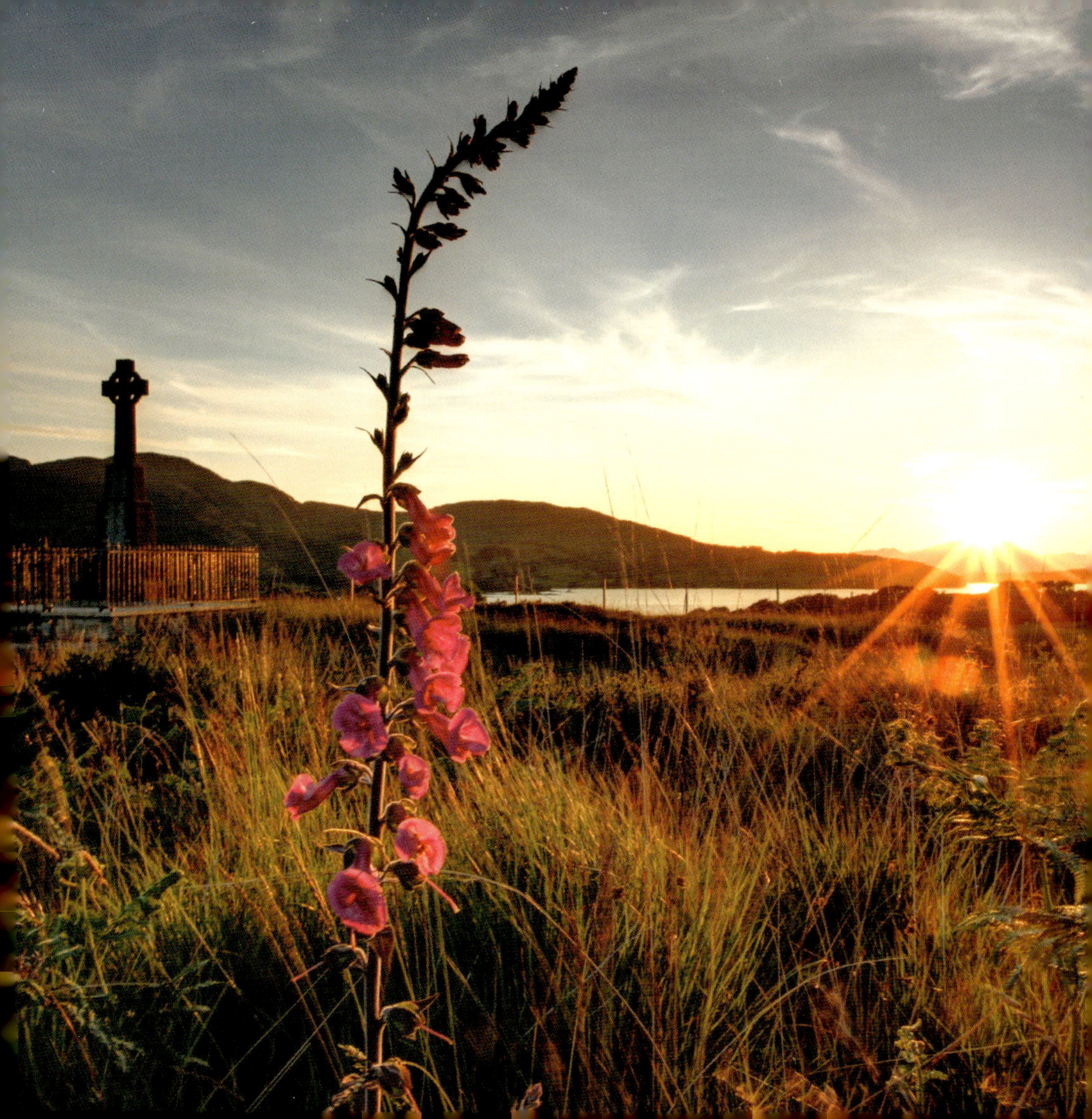

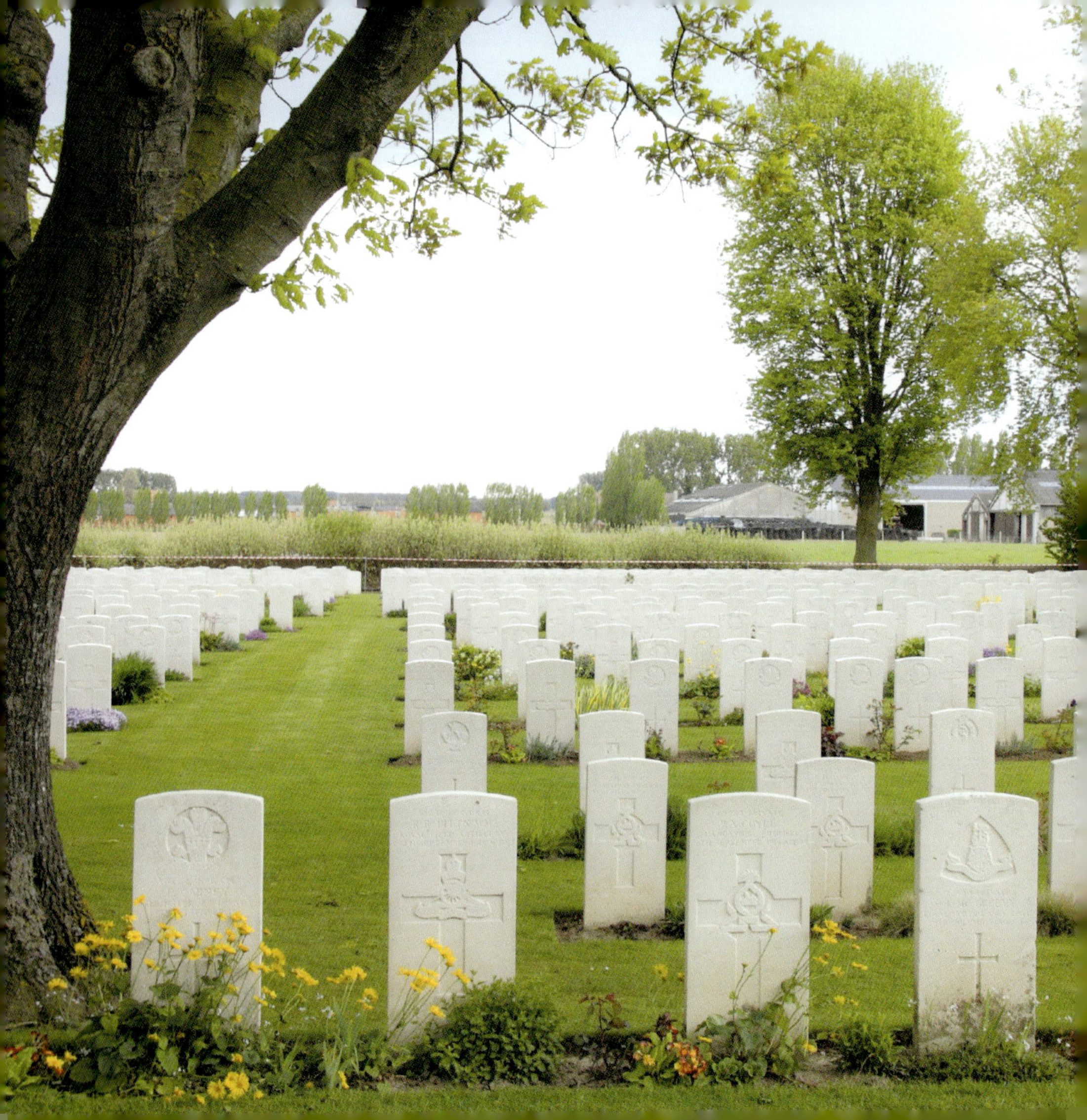

### Yr aberth mawr

O'i wlad aeth i warchffos lom – Ewrob erch,
　　Lle mae'r byd yn storom;
　A'i waed gwin yn y drin drom
　Ni waharddai hwn erddom.

## The great sacrifice

He went from his home country – to a trench
　　Where war rages fiercely;
　Pouring his blood willingly
　For us in battle's fury.

*Vlamertinghe New Military Cemetery, where Ellis John Jones from Trawsfynydd, a young man the same age as Hedd Wyn, is buried*

Hedd Wyn

## Marw oddi cartref

Mae beddrod ei fam yn Nhrawsfynydd,
    Cynefin y gwynt a'r glaw,
Ac yntau ynghwsg ar obennydd
    Ym mynwent yr estron draw.

Bu fyw ag addfwynder a chariad
    Yn llanw'i galon ddi-frad;
Bu farw â serch yn ei lygad
    Ar allor rhyddid ei wlad.

Bu farw a'r byd yn ei drafferth
    Yng nghanol y rhyfel mawr:
Bu farw mor ifanc a phrydferth
    Â chwmwl yn nwylo'r wawr.

Breuddwydiodd am fywyd diwayw
    A'i obaith i gyd yn wyn;
Mor galed, mor anodd oedd marw
    Mor ifanc, mor dlws â hyn.

Ni ddaw gyda'r hafau melynion
    Byth mwy i'w ardal am dro;
Cans mynwent sy'n nhiroedd yr estron
    Ac yntau ynghwsg yn ei gro.

Ac weithian yn erw y marw
    Caed yntau huno mewn hedd;
Boed adain y nef dros ei weddw,
    A dail a rhos dros ei fedd.

*Foel Ddu*

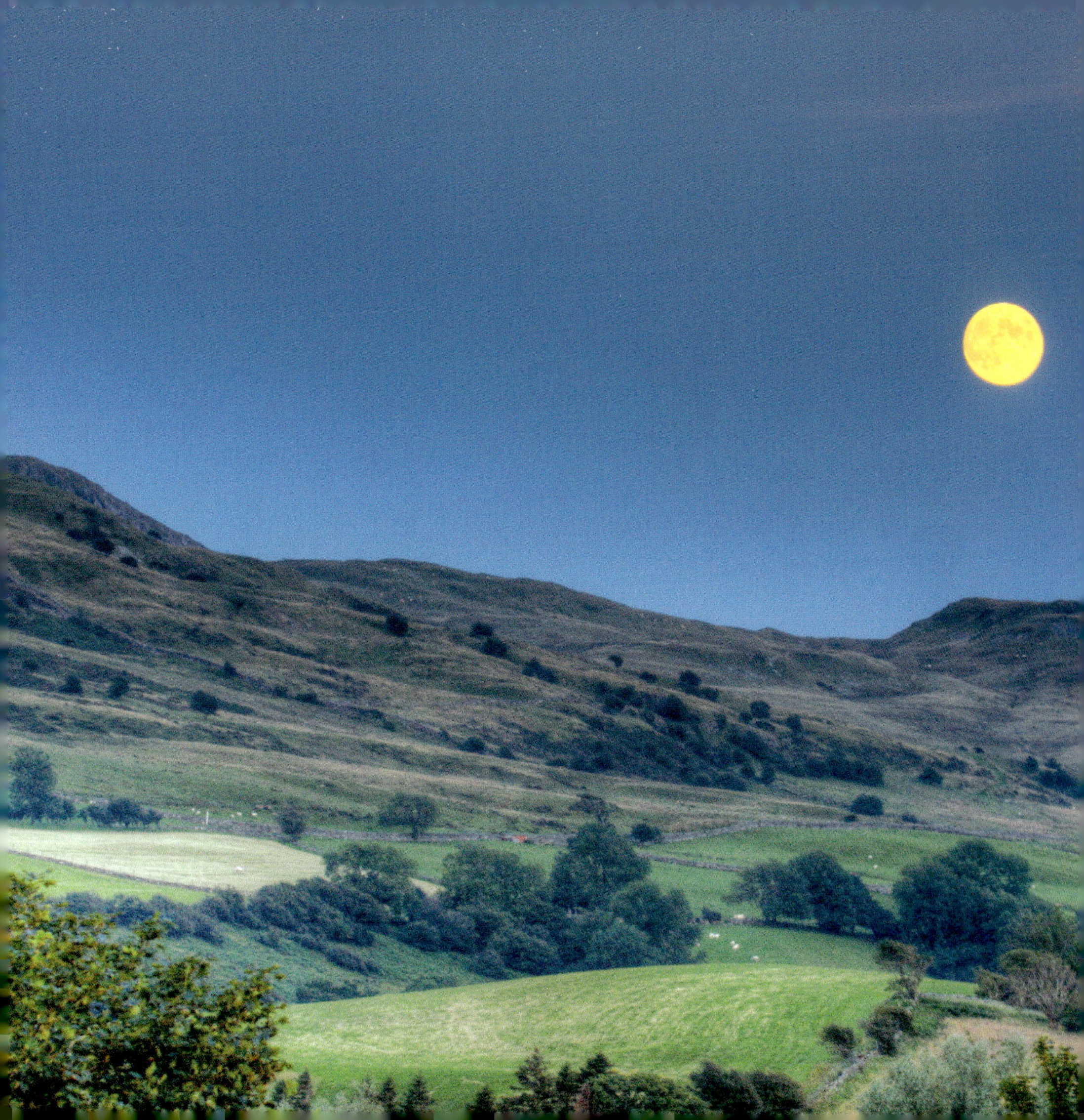

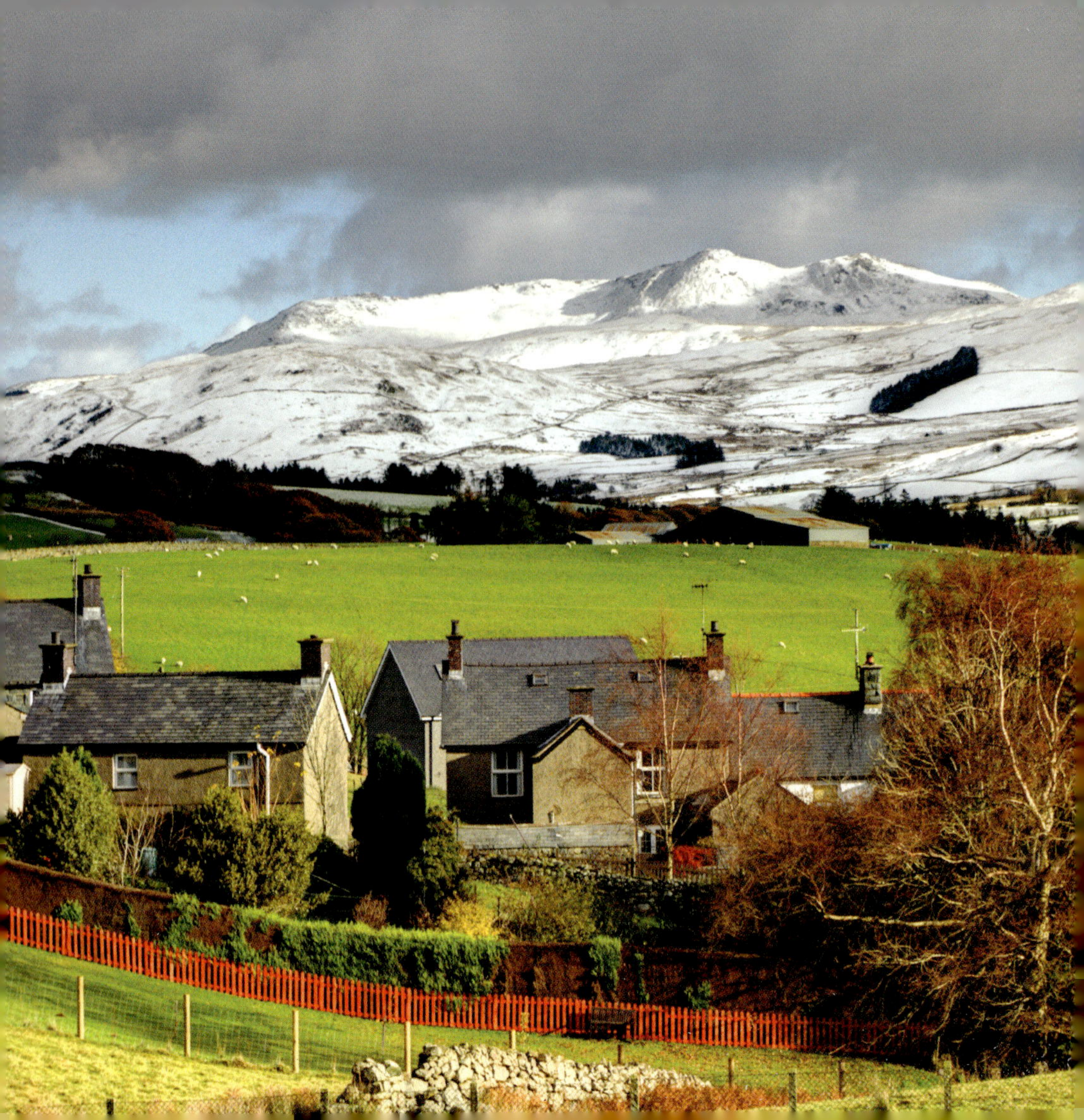

# To die far from home

His mother's tomb is at Trawsfynydd,
    Where the wind and rain hold sway,
As he now asleep on a pillow lies
    In a graveyard far away.

A heart full of love and affection,
    A heart free of guile had he,
With love in his eyes, he gave his life for
    His country's liberty.

He died in the midst of the Great War
    In a world by its troubles torn;
He died as young and as beautiful
    As a cloud in the hands of dawn.

He dreamt of a life without suffering,
    A life full of hope new-sprung;
How hard, and how difficult to die
    As handsome as this, and so young.

No more in the golden summertime
    Will he back to his homeland stray;
For there's a graveyard in a foreign field
    And he lies asleep in its clay.

And now in the acre of the dead
    In tranquility may he repose;
May heaven's wing shelter his widow,
    On his grave, let there be a rose.

*Winter, Arenig*

*Hedd Wyn*

**Y gwahodd**

"Tyrd gyda mi dros y tonnau,"
    Medd llais o'r ystorom bell,
"Fe'th boenaf di â rhosynnau
    A golau y tiroedd maith pell,
    A chwerthin ynysoedd sydd well.

"Os tyr dy long ar y cefnfor
    Ba waeth, bid lawen dy fron;
Mae plasau emrallt fy ngoror
    Yn nyfnder beryl y don,
    Dan lif wylofus y don;

"Os cludir dy gorff tua'r glannau
    Yn llaith dan ewynnau gwyn,
Caiff d'ysbryd drigo'r dyfnderau
    Fel lloer yn nyfnderau'r llyn,
    Fel paladr haul yn y llyn.

"Cyfod dy hwyliau, a dilyn;
    Nac oeda mewn byd mor ffôl;
Cei forio am haf brigfelyn
    A'th hirwallt ar chwyf o'th ôl,
    Fel baner ddu ar dy ôl.

"Gwêl lewych y wenfro ddisglair
    Tros lasdon Iwerydd erch,
Lle'r oeda rhos rhwng y glaswair
    Fel mwynion ddeialau serch,
    Fel dedwydd offeiriaid serch."

# The inviting

"Come with me across the breakers,"
    Says a voice from a storm far away,
"And I'll torment you with roses
    And the light of wide lands far away,
    And the mirth of a fairer cay.

"Should your ship founder on the ocean,
    What of it? May your heart be at ease;
The emerald mansions of my realm
    Are deep in the beryl seas,
    Deep under the weeping seas.

"If your body be borne to the coastline
    All wet on its foamy white bier,
Your spirit can live on in the depths
    Like the moon in the depths of the mere,
    Like a shaft of sunlight in the mere.

"So raise up your sails now, and follow,
    Don't stay in so foolish a world;
You can sail to a golden summer time
    With your hair flying behind you
                           unfurled,
    Like a black flag behind you unfurled.

"Behold across the Atlantic's wave
    An Eden all shining and bright,
Where the roses linger among the grass
    Like sweet sundials of love's delight,
    Like happy priests of love's delight."

*Hedd Wyn*

**Yr arwr** *(Detholiad)*
*Awdl fuddugol y Gadair Ddu yn 1917*

Wylo anniddig dwfn fy mlynyddoedd
A'm gwewyr glywwyd ar lwm greigleoedd,
    Canys Merch y Drycinoedd – oeddwn gynt:
Criwn ym mawrwynt ac oerni moroedd.

Dioer wylwn am na welwn f'anwylyd,
Tywysog meibion gwlad desog mebyd,
    Pan nad oedd un penyd hyd – ein dyddiau,
Ac i'w rhuddem hafau cerddem hefyd.

Un hwyr pan heliodd niwl i'r panylau
Rwydi o wead dieithr y duwiau,
    Mi wybum weld y mab mau – yn troi'n rhydd
O hen fagwyrydd dedwydd ei dadau.

Y llanc a welwn trwy'r gwyll yn cilio
I ddeildre hudol werdd Eldorado,
    O'i ôl bu'r coed yn wylo, – a nentydd
Yn nhawch annedwydd yn ucheneidio.

Y macwy heulog, paham y ciliodd?
Ba ryw hud anwel o'm bro a'i denodd?
    Ei oed a'i eiriau dorrodd, – ac o'i drig
Ddiofal unig efe ddiflannodd.

## The hero (*Extract*)
*The ode that won the Black Chair in 1917*

My years of weeping, deep and stricken,
And my anguish were heard where rocks lie barren,
    For I was the Storm Maiden – and of old
I cried in the tempest and the cold ocean.

Ardently I wept, for lack of seeing
The prince of the land of youth, my darling,
    When our days knew no suffering – and we
Into its ruby summers went strolling.

One dusk, as in hollows the mist collected,
In webs as weird as gods might have braided,
    I saw: my lad departed – the happy
And ancient dwelling-place of his kindred.

I beheld the lad through the dusk going
To Eldorado, green and enchanting;
    As he went, trees were weeping – and streams too
Flowed through a dismal miasma, sighing.

Why did he depart, this radiant youngster?
What drew him from me, what unseen power?
    Breaking word and pledge together – then he
In his carefree home was seen no longer.

*Hedd Wyn*

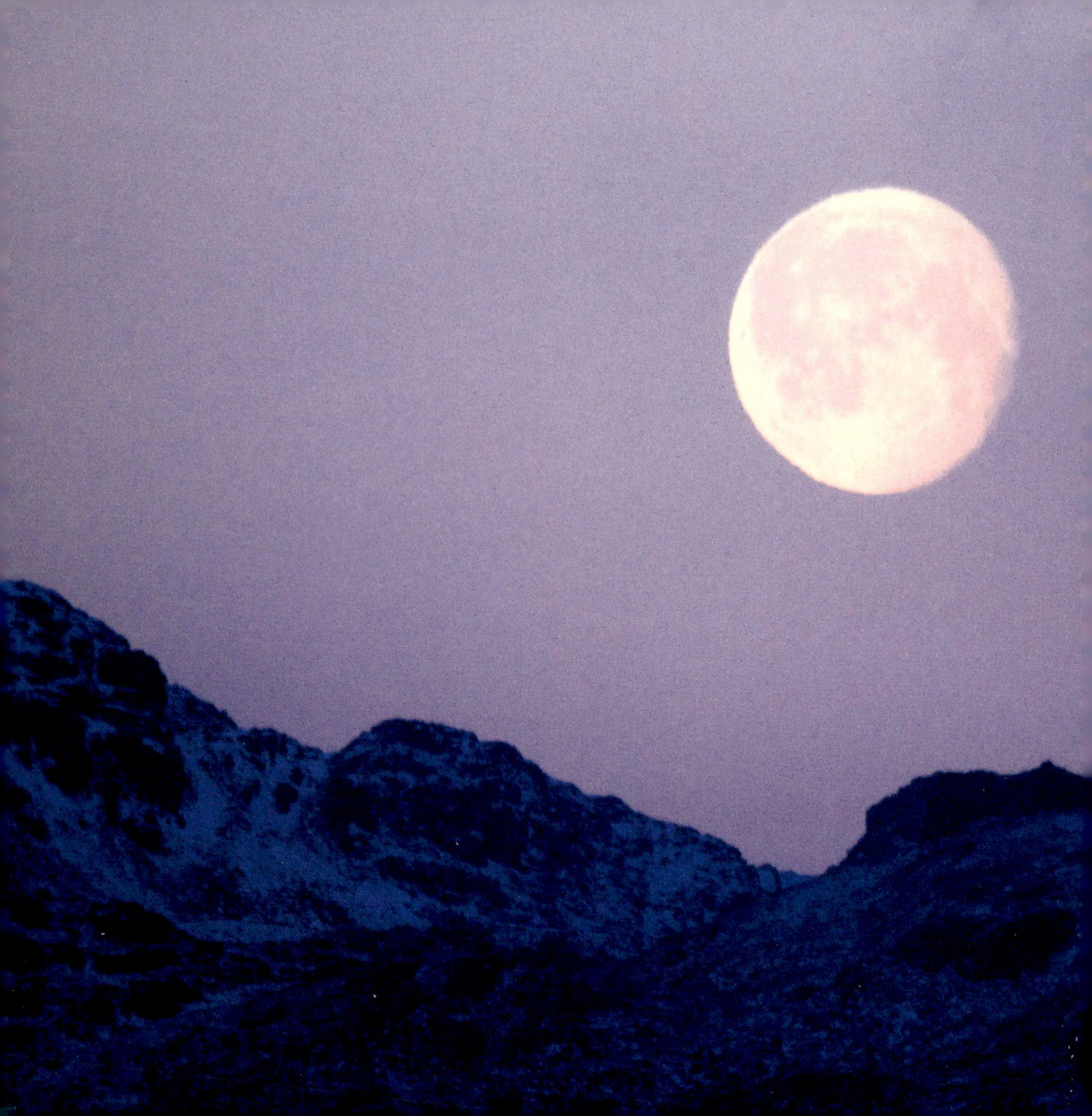

## Atgo

Dim ond lleuad borffor
    Ar fin y mynydd llwm;
A sŵn hen afon Prysor
    Yn canu yn y Cwm.

## A memory

Nought but a purple moon
    Above the moorland hung,
As in the glen old Prysor goes
    Singing as it flows along.

*Above Rhinogydd*

*Hedd Wyn*

# Yr Ysgwrn 2017

Since September 1917, thousands of visitors have flocked to Yr Ysgwrn on pilgrimages in search of the home of Hedd Wyn (*Blessed Peace*). The farm stands on the southern slopes of Cwm Prysor, near Trawsfynydd, This is an open location, a suntrap on a few days of the year, but more usually in the path of driving wind and rain, as described by Hedd Wyn himself. This modern farmhouse became famous as the cradle of the talents of one of Wales' most well-known poets, and as a home to that symbol of the personal achievement and fall of around forty thousand Welshmen lost in the Great War, Y Gadair Ddu (*the Black Chair*). Over the last century, Yr Ysgwrn has become a symbol of the advent of the modern world during that time, and this is now one of Wales' most famous homes.

Regardless of its status in the history and culture of modern Wales, Yr Ysgwrn was always a very ordinary home.

The farmhouse was built in 1830, and nowadays it is legally protected as a Grade II* listed building. It was built from local stone, with its green paintwork imitating the surrounding landscape. The name of William Evans, the maker of the second generation of windows, is etched into one of the small panes of the parlour windows, evidencing the prestige of local craftsmanship. The farmhouse itself is a very attractive building and the stonework suggests a certain tenacity. How apt, as branches of the same family have lived here from the very beginning. Surrounding the farmhouse is a collection of agricultural buildings which tell the story of a way of life: the pig sty, or Tŷ Bach (Little house) as it is called by the family, which housed pigs until the Second World War, and the Beudy Tŷ and Beudy Llwyd cowsheds in which hay was stored hay and cattle wintered. Decreasing use has been made of them in later years, following the building of a modern shed in the 1980s, but the beautiful buildings have survived with their original features intact, including stonework and slate floors.

*1. The parlour, Yr Ysgwrn 2014;*
*2. The kitchen, Yr Ysgwrn 2014;*
*3. Yr Ysgwrn's summer fields, 2016*

*The Shepherd War Poet*

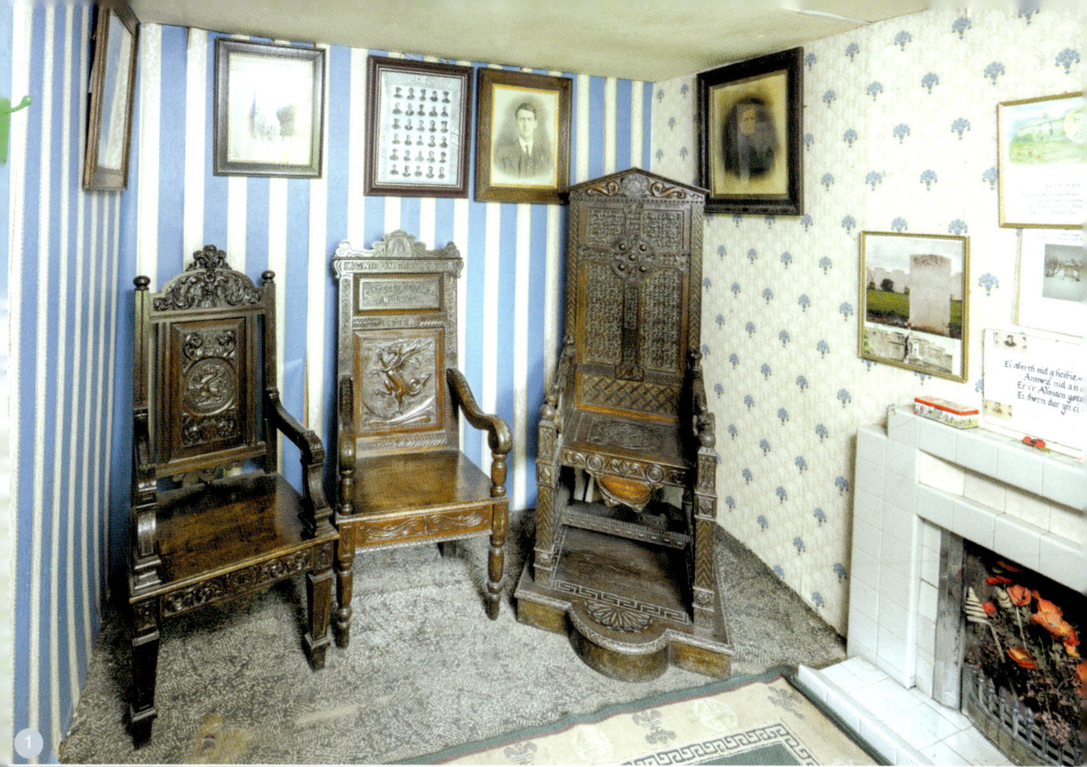

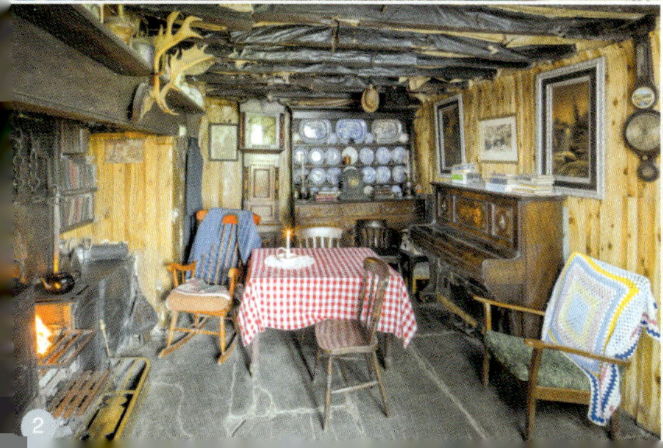

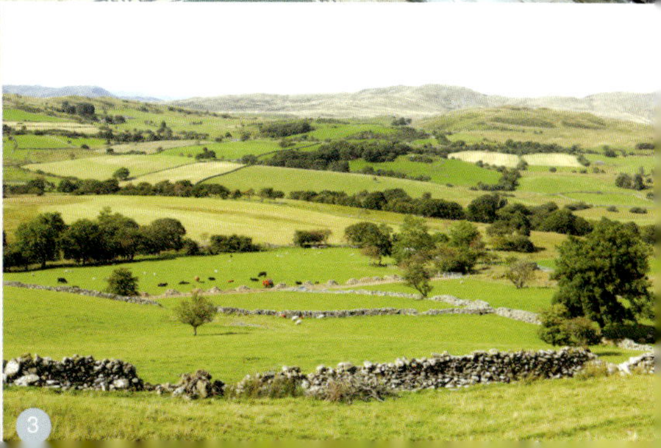

Griffith William, Hedd Wyn's great-great-uncle was the first of the family to live at Yr Ysgwrn, as a tenant in the 1830s. By the 1840s, his nephew Lewis Evans and his wife, Mary, had moved from the Erwddwfr farm in Bronaber to take the tenancy at Yr Ysgwrn and it became home to them and their family of nine children: Sarah (the first), Ellis, Lewis, Edmund (Emwnt), Evan, Morris, Sarah (the second), Mary and Robert.

Evan Evans, son of Lewis, took over at Yr Ysgwrn in 1887, around the time of the death of his mother, Mary. He returned to Yr Ysgwrn, with his wife, also called Mary, and their four-month old son, Ellis, to help Lewis with the running of the farm. Thirteen other children were born to them at Yr Ysgwrn: David (Dafydd), Mary, Kate (Cati), Llywelyn Lewis (the first), Sarah Ann, Magi, Robert Llywelyn (Robin or Bob), Llywelyn Lewis (the second), Evan, Ann and Enid. Life was hard: there were two stillborn children, and both boys named Llywelyn Lewis, as well as Sarah Ann, were lost to disease as infants. The family history of Yr Ysgwrn is shared with families throughout rural Wales.

Life wasn't particularly prosperous at Yr Ysgwrn, but the family had the means to employ a servant. It is likely that local lads who lived at home were the farm hands, but the maids would lodge at Yr Ysgwrn. Their home was a small chamber behind the kitchen, made comfortable by only a bed and a clothes chest and the heat of the chimney for warmth. For some years, two maids were employed at Yr Ysgwrn, until Hedd Wyn's sisters grew old enough to work at home, having left school.

Farming and working the land sustained every generation to live at Yr Ysgwrn. A 168-acre farm, with fields including Rhos Grwm, Cae Llouau Bach and Cae Dan Tŷ, it was home to cattle and sheep, with pigs living in the pigsty and the horses taking their place in the stable, all surrounding the farmhouse. Hens and geese would roam the farmyard and the family would grow crops such as potatoes, carrots and swedes in the fields, and fruit and rhubarb in the garden. The way of life was self-sustaining and, as on all other farms and smallholdings in Wales, little produce was purchased. This was a co-operative community and help was readily available from uncles Lewis, Emwnt and

Robert and from neighbours at the local Bodyfuddai, Plas Capten, Bryn Golau and Fronysgellog farms on important days, such as shearing day, threshing day and during the harvest.

Even though the community and way of life changed during the twentieth century, Yr Ysgwrn continues to be a working farm, with a stock of cattle and sheep, and the agricultural calendar worked for nearly two centuries continues to turn.

Nowadays, the historic cowsheds are open to visitors to Yr Ysgwrn and it is possible to experience some of the history of Yr Ysgwrn and the First World War inside. The special character of both buildings has been preserved by working with the beautiful original features and including them in the interpretation of the building. The Ysgubor Newydd barn is the current agricultural building, a brand-new building developed to service a modern farm, built using environmental best practice. Ysgubor Newydd is sensitively positioned in the landscape: tucked within the topography of the farm, and with a live green roof providing a natural cap on top.

Cattle were milked in the byre. They would be called from the fields with a shout of "*swc, swc, swc*", and the bull would stand quietly among the cows. Milking was the work of Ifan and Bob, two of Hedd Wyn's younger brothers, who would sit on small stools for the job, their father supervising them, daydreaming and smoking his pipe.

There were two buteries at Yr Ysgwrn: Y Bwtri and Bwtri Bellaf. Food was kept cool in Bwtri Bellaf and it was in Y Bwtri that Mary Evans used to churn her butter, which she sold locally.

Many changes have happened since, and milking has ceased altogether at Yr Ysgwrn. One feature of Yr Ysgwrn that saw very little change over the last century is the *cegin* (kitchen). The *cegin* was the heart of the home and this is where the family welcomed neighbours and friends. This is also where Hedd Wyn learnt to compose poetry from his father, Evan, a country poet who wrote poems about local events. Lined with twenty-six layers of wallpaper until recently, the *cegin* is a testament to the special culture of rural Wales. The dresser and clock, situated in the *cegin*, would be the most important possessions in any Welsh home. At Yr Ysgwrn they are accompanied by other beautiful objects, including a traditional Welsh food cupboard, a slate-lined cold cupboard, a barometer, a piano and a traditional 1880s kitchen range. The footsteps of generations of the family are ingrained in the slate floor, and the overhead beams, furnished with hooks for the joints of ham, demonstrate how productive this farm was. Opposite, on bookshelves above the range, are rows of books of all kinds, from anthologies of poetry to prayer books and cowboy novels, conveying a culturally eclectic home. Self-education was very important, as Hedd Wyn received an intermittent school education. If anything more important than the lessons demanded his time at home, that is where he stayed. The chapel and Sunday school were therefore essential to quench some of his thirst for information on the world around him.

The piano itself is an unusual feature of the *cegin* at Yr Ysgwrn, as it was moved there to make room in the parlour for the bardic Chairs won by Hedd Wyn between 1907 and 1915. The Chairs are symbols of the family's pride in the achievements of their son: each prize had to go into the parlour, the best room in the house.

*Y Gadair Ddu* was also kept in the parlour since its arrival at Yr Ysgwrn from Birkenhead in September 1917 and, to most visitors, seeing this remarkable Chair is the pinnacle of their visit to Yr Ysgwrn. Since 1917, the family attempted to continue their a way of life in the face of a steady flow of visitors keen to meet them and to pay their respects to their son, brother and uncle. Evan and Mary Evans, Bob and Evan Evans and Ellis and Gerald Williams, with the assistance of their extended family have been responsible for keeping the door of Yr Ysgwrn open, and in 2012 this responsibility was transferred to the Snowdonia National Park Authority. With the support of a heritage grant received from the Heritage Lottery Fund in 2014, the National Park Authority has been able to continue a way of life by sustaining the working farm, protecting the buildings and heritage and continuing to welcome visitors from throughout Wales and beyond. The challenge now is to keep the door open and to safeguard those characteristics that have made Yr Ysgwrn such a special place to generations of visitors, enabling them to get under the skin of this remarkable place.